In Search of The BRIDE

THE KING IS LOOKING FOR THE ONE

DAVID O'BRIEN

ISBN: 978-1-960245-06-9

Abbreviations:

NKJV – New King James Version
N.A.S.B. – New American Standard Bible
E.S.V. – English Standard Version
N.I.V. – New International Version

Additions of literal meanings in Scripture passages are made in brackets.

Blue Diamond Bookhouse

www.BlueDiamondBookhouse.com

“He who has the bride is the bridegroom”

–the prophet John, who first introduced Jesus to the world

–John 3:29, The Set Apart Book

Dedication

For the Bride, for the Bridegroom

Contents

Questions about The Bride vi

1. The Submissiveness of the Lamb 1
2. The Bride is Taken Out of The Body 17
3. How She Learns Her Identity 21
4. She Becomes Radiant 25
5. She Prepares Herself with Glory 29
6. Her Self-Denial, Pleasure & Service 35
7. She Becomes Absolutely Distinctive 43
8. The Bride's Maturity 55
9. Characteristics of Marriage & Purity 59
10. She Answers the Calls 73
11. How She Dwells Above the Earth 77
12. She Overcomes Religion 83
13. She Delights in Meditation 89
14. She Discovers the Kingdom 93
15. How The Bride Endures 101
16. How She Sees Jesus 109
17. She Shines in the Darkest of Places 113
18. She Overcomes the Cliff & Rut 119
19. How She Overcomes in the Wilderness 127
20. Something Happens to Her in the Desert 133
21. You Don't Know the Bride 137

More Life Changing Resources 149

Questions about The Bride

Where can the glorious "The Bride of the Lamb" be found?

She is found by seeing the glory of the Lord, as in a mirror. As you find it you will see diamonds of her splendor in your own spirit. These have been there all along waiting for your discovery.

Where is the Bride now?

The Bride is *in* the Body now and becomes visible as she sees her glory. She is in a secret place, transfiguring till her time of full revelation.

What does the Bridegroom think of the Bride?

For the Bridegroom, her sweetness is *entirely* worth the wait.

Is the Bride always victorious?

The Bride has been bullied. But She will stand upright, stronger than any bystander would ever predict. She is undefeatable.

The Bride has the unique ability to turn *her problems into pearls.* A clam's response to a foreign irritant eventually forms a beautiful pearl. In the end, the Bride will display a *necklace of pearls*.

What will this book do for me?

This book contains the Bridegroom's image and a glorious invitation upward for the Bride. Come and drink, enter deeply and cleanse yourself in this refreshing, living water and display an even greater *glory.*

—David O'Brien

Chapter 1

The Submissiveness of The Lamb

Characteristic to the Bride of the Lamb is that she is *compatible* with the Lamb, "bone of his bone and flesh of his flesh" (See Genesis 2:23). And the lamb, by nature, is submissive.

[Isaiah 53:7 NKJV] 7 He was oppressed and He was afflicted, Yet He opened not His mouth; He was led as a lamb to the slaughter, And as a sheep before its shearers is silent, So He opened not His mouth.

The Old Testament, as well as physical creation, is full of analogies to the True life that is in The Anointed King ("Christ"). In the Book of Esther, two queens were displayed, one having the adornment of submissiveness.

Queen Vashti was the original wife of King Ahasuerus. Though she was "beautiful to behold," she lacked the inner characteristic of submissiveness—a major part of the "inner beauty of the heart" (see 1 Peter 3:4). She was independent. Her heart was lifted up in pride. And this disqualified her from being Queen to the King:

[Esther 1:2-20 N.A.S.B.] 2 In those days as King Ahasuerus sat on his royal throne which [was] at the citadel in Susa, 3 in the third year of his reign he held a banquet for all his officials and attendants, the army [officers] of Persia and Media, the nobles and the officials of his provinces, in his presence. 4 At that time he displayed the riches of his royal glory and the splendor of his great majesty for many days, 180 days. 5 When these days were finished, the king held a banquet lasting seven days for all the people who were present at the citadel in Susa, from the greatest

to the least, in the courtyard of the garden of the king's palace. 6
[There were curtains of] fine white and violet linen held by cords
of fine purple linen on silver rings and marble columns, [and]
couches of gold and silver on a mosaic floor of porphyry, marble,
mother-of-pearl, and mineral stones. 7 Drinks were served in
golden vessels of various kinds, and the royal wine was plentiful
in proportion to the king's bounty. 8 But the drinking was [done]
according to the [royal] law; there was no compulsion, for so the
king had given orders to each official of his household, that he
was to do as each person pleased. 9 Queen Vashti also held a
banquet for the women in the palace which belonged to King
Ahasuerus. 10 On the seventh day, when the heart of the king was
cheerful with wine, he ordered Mehuman, Biztha, Harbona,
Bigtha, Abagtha, Zethar, and Carkas, the seven eunuchs who
served in the presence of King Ahasuerus, 11 to bring Queen
Vashti before the king with [her] royal turban in order to display
her beauty to the people and the officials, for she was beautiful.
12 But Queen Vashti refused to come at the king's order
delivered by the eunuchs. So the king became very angry, and his
wrath burned within him. 13 Then the king said to the wise men
who understood the times—for it was the custom of the king [to
speak] this way before all who knew [Persian] law and justice 14
and were close to him, [namely,] Carshena, Shethar, Admatha,
Tarshish, Meres, Marsena, and Memucan, the seven officials of
Persia and Media who had access to the king's presence and sat
in the first place in the kingdom— 15 "According to law, what is
to be done with Queen Vashti, since she did not obey the
command of King Ahasuerus delivered by the eunuchs?" 16 And
in the presence of the king and the [other] officials, Memucan
said, "Queen Vashti has wronged not only the king but [also] all
the officials and all the peoples who are in all the provinces of
King Ahasuerus. 17 "For the queen's conduct will become known
to all the women so as to make their own husbands despicable in
their sight, when they say, 'King Ahasuerus commanded that
Queen Vashti be brought in to his presence, but she did not
come.' 18 "And this day the wives of the officials of Persia and
Media who have heard about the queen's conduct will talk [about
it] to all the king's officials, and there will be plenty of contempt
and anger. 19 "If it pleases the king, let a royal edict be issued by
him and let it be written in the laws of Persia and Media so that it

cannot be repealed, that Vashti may not come into the presence of King Ahasuerus, and let the king give her royal position to another who is more worthy than she. 20 "When the king's edict which he will make is heard throughout his kingdom, great as it is, then all women will give honor to their husbands, great and small."

Now look at Esther's example. She yielded to both Mordecai's instructions and to "everything" the chief eunuch told her (Esther 2:10,15,20) in her preparation to be presented before the King. That ONE characteristic of submissiveness set her apart from *all* of the other potential queens. This is what the King of Kings is seeking among his People today.

When Esther was queen, she rightfully possessed "half the kingdom" (see Esther 5:3,6, 7:2), but she maintained an approach of submissiveness before the king—something Queen Vashti lost.

I've travelled around the world and seen culture after culture in country after country. One thing characteristic, regardless of race, is that men (males) are strong physically. Part of the glory God gave them is their physical strength.

[Matthew 19:4 N.A.S.B.] 4 [Jesus] said...He who created [them] from the beginning MADE THEM MALE AND FEMALE

Samson is an example of a man who used physical strength to defend and protect Israel, back when there weren't sophisticated military weapons. This was not his natural strength, but nonetheless, God gave such physical might, for physical war, to a man. Why?

Women, on the other hand, were created in some ways stronger than men *internally*. Eve was given as a help to Adam, so she was obviously stronger (you don't send someone weaker to go help someone)! The two came from the same Man. Therefore, they were and always would be equal in nature, and they were given the same commission. So why the distinction in role and responsibility?

Male and female were both part of the first Man, to start. Now, in the Chosen King Jesus, there no longer exists male and female, according to spirit. So why the continuing distinction? Why did God physically make all men strong and all women beautiful?

In all cultures of the earth, women are beautiful. They carry the image of the beauty of the Creator, and that is known and seen in all parts of the earth, just as men have physical strength. Some men carry some beauty also, for example, Absalom, one of King David's sons, according to the original Hebrew (see 2 Samuel 14:25, literal). But *all* women carry beauty. All.

All men, no matter how small or weak, if they exercise physically will begin to show physical strength. It's built into the fibers of their bodies' makeup. Some women are very strong physically and develop a lethal, protective instinct. But they also carry beauty, definitely, and that's a very valuable thing.

The souls of men and women are different also, as are the physical brains, emotions, etc.

God made the original man to represent him and to spread his Kingdom over the earth, and he separated "wo-man" (or "out of man") to bring about a complementary team. The two fit together like two puzzle pieces, each one's strengths complementing the other's weaknesses, perfectly. In the covenant of marriage, this relationship can become splendid. And though it is by far the most amazing relationship in all of physical creation, it's still only surface level.

The deeper reason God "made them male and female" was to give an analogy for God's People of the co-relationship between the Chosen King Jesus and his Bride to be.

[Ephesians 5:28-32 N.A.S.B.] 28 So husbands also ought to love their own wives as their own bodies. He who loves his own wife loves himself; 29 for no one ever hated his own flesh, but nourishes and cherishes it, just as [The Anointed King] also [does] the [Legislature], 30 because we are parts of His body. 31 FOR THIS REASON A MAN SHALL LEAVE HIS FATHER AND HIS MOTHER AND BE JOINED TO HIS WIFE, AND THE TWO SHALL BECOME ONE FLESH. 32 This mystery is great; but I am speaking with reference to [The Anointed King] [that is, The Anointed King] and the [Legislature].

The term, "submit" in English sometimes creates a picture of force or domination. The original Greek and Hebrew of the Bible carries the meaning of "*yield*," which by definition cannot be forced. If it's forced it's not yielding or true "submission". Yielding is an internal choice.

Why did God command wives (female) to yield to the leadership of their husbands (male)? It was not out of inequality. Not only have we established that God created them equal in nature, the Chosen King Jesus also died for each, proving God's equal love for each and the equal *value* of each. And in The Anointed King, where "There is no male or female," they were given the same "Great Commission." This commission is to go evangelize and make disciples worldwide, as members of the same Body of the Chosen King.

The distinction given to physical male and female is in abilities and responsibilities within the marriage relationship. Together they make up the complete image of God. He is the master artist, and each part of his creation is a masterpiece. Each boy and girl should be celebrated, their nature and value celebrated, their distinctive sex celebrated. And their individuality which makes them different than any other person on earth should be celebrated also.

Again, why the specific command for wives to "submit" to their husbands, to voluntarily yield to them? Being submissive does not mean being ignorant. Those of us being groomed collectively as the wife of the Lamb will accept what God says *and* seek to find out why. He has answers for you, and he's not threatened by your asking.

Here are several reasons. First, women are stronger than men, in many ways internally. Yielding is a check, a guard, for self-control. As the banks of a river channel its power, yielding allows the power vested in women to benefit the world.

Second, men are natural protectors of women because of their physical strength. They have a natural radar for physical danger against their wives and families and a natural defensive instinct that will cause a good man to die defending them. The authority of governments and of husbands is first and foremost given to provide protection.

Another reason is that the destiny of woman is more glorious than man's. Woman was hidden in man to start and brought out at the end as the pinnacle of creation, the top, the ultimate. She was given a unique glory and a unique destiny. To achieve that high, high destiny in God's plan requires unique grace and exaltation. How does a woman obtain that? Partly by yielding, by submissiveness—the gentleness of the sheep nature. This is how she can access more grace.

[1 Peter 5:5 NKJV] 5 ..."God resists the proud, but gives grace to the humble."

[Matthew 23:12 NKJV] 12 "And whoever exalts himself will be humbled, and he who humbles himself will be exalted.

[Revelation 5:5-6 NKJV] 5 But one of the elders said to me, "Do not weep. Behold, the Lion of the tribe of Judah, the Root of David, has prevailed…" 6 And I looked, and behold, in the midst of the throne and of the four living creatures, and in the midst of the elders, stood a Lamb as though it had been slain...

Another reason for yielding is to illustrate, as an analogy, the relationship between the Chosen King and his compatible, "Bride of the Lamb."

[Ephesians 5:24 NKJV] 24 Therefore, just as the [Legislature] is subject to [The Anointed King], so [let] the wives [be] to their own husbands in everything.

Because the physical relationship is an analogy, the Father wants women to yield to their husbands, as the Body yields to the Head. And Husbands play a big part in this representation also.

As head, husbands are to receive input from and respond to the body. A husband should become uber sensitive to his wife's needs—emotional, physical, and other needs—like being able to hear a pin drop from far away, and he should run to make sure they are met. This is like the Chosen King treats us, his Body.

This is not to say that earthly husbands should not also yield to their wives. Males do that very well, actually, and pretty often as wives typically give commands easily. For males, the failure is often in *not* commanding and protecting their households. Adam failed as a *leader*. He also failed to *cover* Eve after they fell; men need to learn to lead well, in the fear of God, and to love their wives, putting their interests first and laying down their lives for them.

[Ephesians 5:25, 28-29 NKJV] 25 Husbands, love your wives, just as [The Anointed King] also loved the [Legislature] and gave Himself for her… 28 So husbands ought to love their own wives as their own bodies; he who loves his wife loves himself. 29 For no one ever hated his own flesh, but nourishes and cherishes it, just as the Lord [does] the [Legislature].

Women, on the other hand, sometimes do find yielding to their husband difficult (especially if he's an incompetent or evil one). They can often yield easier to a boss than to their husbands at home.

Eve went rogue in the Garden. She trusted her own ability to evaluate things, and this is how she got in trouble. So for a woman to lay down independence to *trust* and *yield to* a husband, in view of God—this displays the nature of the Lamb. This is incense to God. This brings his grace and exaltation, every time (see 1 Peter 2:20).

So yielding, in the fear of God (not man), is the *ultimate* protection. Without it, we're vulnerable, like Proverbs reveals:

[Proverbs 27:8 NKJV] 8 Like a bird that wanders from its nest is a man [that is, a human] who wanders from his place.

But on the other hand, look at Sarah's example:

[1 Peter 3:3-6 NKJV] 3 Do not let your adornment be merely outward—arranging the hair, wearing gold, or putting on [fine] apparel—[1] 4 rather [let it be] the hidden person of the heart, with the incorruptible [beauty] of a gentle and quiet spirit, which is very precious in the sight of God. 5 For in this manner, in former times, the holy women who trusted in God also adorned themselves, being submissive to their own husbands, 6 as Sarah obeyed Abraham, calling him lord, whose daughters you are if you do good and are not afraid with any terror.

This kind of trust in God and yielding releases *ultimate* strength. It is a display of childlike faith.

In Sarah's case, Abraham had told her to only tell people she was his sister, not his wife (which was partly true). This was out of fear of man, a weakness in Abraham. But because Sarah obeyed him, without any fear, God was able to protect her supernaturally from Abimelech. Look what happened as a direct result:

[Genesis 20:2-3, 7-8, 14, 17-18 NKJV] 2 Now Abraham said of Sarah his wife, "She [is] my sister." And Abimelech king of Gerar sent and took Sarah. 3 But God came to Abimelech in a dream by night, and said to him, "Indeed you [are] a dead man because of the woman whom you have taken, for she [is] a man's wife." ... 7

---

1 That is *an* adornment, but the lowest level. The daughters of God have an internal adornment they can put on, over all of that

"Now therefore, restore the man's wife; for he [is] a prophet, and he will pray for you and you shall live. But if you do not restore [her], know that you shall surely die, you and all who [are] yours." 8 So Abimelech rose early in the morning, called all his servants, and told all these things in their hearing; and the men were very much afraid. ... 14 Then Abimelech took sheep, oxen, and male and female servants, and gave [them] to Abraham; and he restored Sarah his wife to him. ... 17 So Abraham prayed to God; and God healed Abimelech, his wife, and his female servants. Then they bore [children]; 18 for the LORD had closed up all the wombs of the house of Abimelech because of Sarah, Abraham's wife.

The wife of the Lamb knows when to yield. The Lord Jesus himself yielded to the Father in the Garden, against the full persuasion of his soul:

[John 12:27-28 NKJV] 27 "Now My soul is troubled, and what shall I say? 'Father, save Me from this hour'? But for this purpose I came to this hour. 28 "Father, glorify Your name." Then a voice came from heaven, [saying], "I have both glorified [it] and will glorify [it] again."

[Luke 22:42 NKJV] 42 [Jesus said:] "Father, if it is Your will, take this cup away from Me; nevertheless not My will, but Yours, be done."

The Bride of the Lamb learns to do the same. It is part of her preparation to reign with him on the throne of glory. He did not achieve that throne by self-exaltation. He humbled himself and God exalted him up to it.

The Bride of the Lamb will not yield to just anyone, anytime. She knows who not to submit to also. Just as Esther did not submit to Haman and the evil law that went against God's purposes, the Bride knows when and *how* to stand up. We don't yield to the devil.

The Lamb himself broke religious ideologies and traditions fairly regularly. He would not yield to man's human traditions when they went against his Father's. But even this he did while maintaining an attitude of submissiveness and gentleness (see Matthew 17:27 and 23:1-3). He was not reckless. He respected authorities (see Luke 2:51), but he did not give in to tyrants, intimidation, or manipulation (see Luke 13:32). He was like a lamb under the guidance of the dove-like Spirit.

The Bride can see through human, religious, counterfeit authority. She knows *her* authority, sharing the throne with the Anointed King, far above all. And yet she maintains the submissiveness of a servant while on earth. Even when openly disobeying human abuse of authority, she maintains her lamb-like submissiveness.

[Acts 4:13-20 NKJV] 13 Now when they saw the boldness of Peter and John, and perceived that they were uneducated and untrained men, they marveled. And they realized that they had been with Jesus. 14 And seeing the man who had been healed standing with them, they could say nothing against it. 15 But when they had commanded them to go aside out of the council, they conferred among themselves, 16 saying, "What shall we do to these men? For, indeed, that a notable miracle has been done through them [is] evident to all who dwell in Jerusalem, and we cannot deny [it]. 17 "But so that it spreads no further among the people, let us severely threaten them, that from now on they speak to no man in this name." 18 So they called them and commanded them not to speak at all nor teach in the name of Jesus. 19 But Peter and John answered and said to them, "Whether it is right in the sight of God to listen to you more than to God, you judge. 20 "For we cannot but speak the things which we have seen and heard."

[Act 5:16-29 NKJV] 16 Also a multitude gathered from the surrounding cities to Jerusalem, bringing sick people and those who were tormented by unclean spirits, and they were all healed. 17 Then the high priest rose up, and all those who [were] with him (which is the sect of the Sadducees), and they were filled with indignation, 18 and laid their hands on the apostles and put them in the common prison. 19 But at night an angel of the Lord opened the prison doors and brought them out, and said, 20 "Go, stand in the temple and speak to the people all the words of this life." 21 And when they heard [that], they entered the temple early in the morning and taught. But the high priest and those with him came and called the council together, with all the elders of the children of Israel, and sent to the prison to have them brought. 22 But when the officers came and did not find them in

the prison, they returned and reported, 23 saying, "Indeed we found the prison shut securely, and the guards standing outside before the doors; but when we opened them, we found no one inside!" 24 Now when the high priest, the captain of the temple, and the chief priests heard these things, they wondered what the outcome would be. 25 So one came and told them, saying, "Look, the men whom you put in prison are standing in the temple and teaching the people!" 26 Then the captain went with the officers and brought them without violence, for they feared the people, lest they should be stoned. 27 And when they had brought them, they set [them] before the council. And the high priest asked them, 28 saying, "Did we not strictly command you not to teach in this name? And look, you have filled Jerusalem with your doctrine, and intend to bring this Man's blood on us!" 29 But Peter and the [other] apostles answered and said: "We ought to obey God rather than men.

The Bride knows to submit to human governments. She has no problem with this and actually enjoys it, as it is congruent with her Lamb nature.

[Romans 13:1-7 NKJV] 1 Let every soul be subject to the governing authorities. For there is no authority except from God, and the authorities that exist are appointed by God. 2 Therefore whoever resists the authority resists the ordinance of God, and those who resist will bring judgment on themselves. 3 For rulers are not a terror to good works, but to evil. Do you want to be unafraid of the authority? Do what is good, and you will have praise from the same. 4 For he is God's minister to you for good. But if you do evil, be afraid; for he does not bear the sword in vain; for he is God's minister, an avenger to [execute] wrath on him who practices evil. 5 Therefore [you] must be subject, not only because of wrath but also for conscience' sake. 6 For because of this you also pay taxes, for they are God's ministers attending continually to this very thing. 7 Render therefore to all their due: taxes to whom taxes [are due], customs to whom customs, fear to whom fear, honor to whom honor.

[1 Peter 2:12-17 NKJV] 12 having your conduct honorable among the Gentiles, that when they speak against you as evildoers, they

may, by [your] good works which they observe, glorify God in the day of visitation. 13 Therefore submit yourselves to every ordinance of man for the Lord's sake, whether to the king as supreme, 14 or to governors, as to those who are sent by him for the punishment of evildoers and [for the] praise of those who do good. 15 For this is the will of God, that by doing good you may put to silence the ignorance of foolish men— 16 as free, yet not using liberty as a cloak for vice, but as bondservants of God. 17 Honor all [people]. Love the brotherhood. Fear God. Honor the king.

She also knows when *NOT* to bend the knee but to stand straight up, obstinate before evil and misguided leaders. She will not bow, and the fire of the enemy's anger cannot burn Her.

[Daniel 3:12-19 NKJV] 12 "There are certain Jews whom you have set over the affairs of the province of Babylon: Shadrach, Meshach, and Abed-Nego; these men, O king, have not paid due regard to you. They do not serve your gods or worship the gold image which you have set up." 13 Then Nebuchadnezzar, in rage and fury, gave the command to bring Shadrach, Meshach, and Abed-Nego. So they brought these men before the king. 14 Nebuchadnezzar spoke, saying to them, "[Is it] true, Shadrach, Meshach, and Abed-Nego, [that] you do not serve my gods or worship the gold image which I have set up? 15 "Now if you are ready at the time you hear the sound of the horn, flute, harp, lyre, [and] psaltery, in symphony with all kinds of music, and you fall down and worship the image which I have made, [good]! But if you do not worship, you shall be cast immediately into the midst of a burning fiery furnace. And who [is] the god who will deliver you from my hands?" 16 Shadrach, Meshach, and Abed-Nego answered and said to the king, "O Nebuchadnezzar, we have no need to answer you in this matter. 17 "If that [is the case], our God whom we serve is able to deliver us from the burning fiery furnace, and He will deliver [us] from your hand, O king. 18 "But if not, let it be known to you, O king, that we do not serve your gods, nor will we worship the gold image which you have set up." 19 Then Nebuchadnezzar was full of fury, and the expression on his face changed toward Shadrach, Meshach, and Abed-Nego. He spoke and commanded that they heat the

furnace seven times more than it was usually heated.

The maturing Body of The Anointed King, while still naïve, does not always get this. They can risk their place in the Bride by yielding to the wrong people, those strong through religion. Paul had to say these things to some of his children in the faith:

[2Corinthians 11:19-21 N.I.V.] 19 You gladly put up with fools since you are so "wise"! 20 In fact, you even put up with anyone who enslaves you or exploits you or takes advantage of you or puts on airs or slaps you in the face. 21 To my shame I admit that we were too "weak" for that!...

[2Corinthians 11:2-4 E.S.V.] 2 For I feel a divine jealousy for you, since I betrothed you to one husband, to present you as a pure virgin to [The Anointed King]. 3 But I am afraid that as the serpent deceived Eve by his cunning, your thoughts will be led astray from a sincere and pure devotion to [The Anointed King]. 4 For if someone comes and proclaims another Jesus than the one we proclaimed, or if you receive a different spirit from the one you received, or if you accept a different gospel from the one you accepted, you put up with it...

[Galatians 1:6-7 E.S.V.] 6 I am astonished that you are so quickly deserting him who called you in the grace of [The Anointed King] and are turning to a different gospel— 7 not that there is another one, but there are some who trouble you and want to distort the gospel of [The Anointed King].

But the Bride: she not only yields to the Head, she knows who to stay away from:

[John 10:2-5 E.S.V.] 2 But he who enters by the door is the shepherd of the sheep. 3 To him the gatekeeper opens. The sheep hear his voice, and he calls his own sheep by name and leads them out. 4 When he has brought out all his own, he goes before them, and the sheep follow him, for they know his voice. 5 A stranger they will not follow, but they will flee from him, for they do not know the voice of strangers."

The Bride of the Lamb does not yield to manipulation or intimidation. She can't do that AND keep her garments clean, so she learns to see through those deceptions. She learns to be both "shrewd and innocent" in the world (see Matthew 10:16).

As we yield to the voice of the Spirit of Truth, over and over, season after season, we are being prepared for acceptance as the Bride of the King. This is just as Esther yielded to the chief eunuch. She yielded during 12 months of beauty treatment: six months with spices and ointments (representing ease and comfort) and six months with myrrh (representing opposition) (see Esther 2:12). Yielding in everything—positive and negative—is preparing us for that Day. He is working out everything for our good as we love and obey him (see Romans 8:28), We are growing up "in everything unto him who is the Head" (see Ephesians 4:13).

This is the greatest adventure, the greatest process of promotion and the greatest privilege of anyone in all of history, in all creation.

Why did Queen Vashti lose her exalted position? Why do some within the Body of the Chosen King not want to yield to God's designated authorities? The inner resistance is like a steel rod, preventing a person from being able to bend.

One reason may come from being raised in an oppressive environment. Jesus said, "The Gentiles lord it over one another…" (see Matthew 20:25-26). In that environment, a person is told that God wants absolute submission to authority figures within in a system, such as religion, family, or government. People strive for perfection in that environment, all the while experiencing pride and oppression by those "above" them, not servanthood. It's painful to the soul, and Jesus said, "this must not be so among you."

Jesus brought the Kingdom culture to earth. It still may not be easy to submit to authority sometimes, when the soul's desire for independence reveals itself, but the authorities in the Kingdom serve and sacrifice to *lift up* those under their charge. To verbally remove oneself from such an oppressive system (as in fact you are in the Anointed King's Body), to recognize one's individual worth outside of that "ladder" system, and to forgive people individually for past oppression—these will heal the heart, empower the eyes, and allow a person to operate freely in *their own glory*, regardless of others.

Another reason for inability to yield is fear of being oppressed by leadership. This is alleviated by submitting, "in the fear of the Lord," in other words, seeing the Lord rather than the authority he put in place.

It is putting one's trust in the Lord.

Fear of being belittled by leadership is alleviated by choosing to be the servant, in whatever environment you're in—voluntarily giving up your "rights," like the Anointed King did (see John 13, Philippians 2). Taking the lowest place, which, as he revealed, is actually the highest place in the Kingdom. When you're voluntarily at the lowest place, no man can put you there by oppression.

[Mark 10:42-45 ESV] 42 And Jesus called them to him and said to them, "You know that those who are considered rulers of the Gentiles lord it over them, and their great ones exercise authority over them. 43 But it shall not be so among you. But whoever would be great among you must be your servant, 44 and whoever would be first among you must be slave of all. 45 For even the Son of Man came not to be served but to serve, and to give his life as a ransom for many."

[1 Peter 5:6-7 E.S.V.] 6 Humble yourselves, therefore, under the mighty hand of God so that at the proper time he may exalt you, 7 casting all your anxieties on him, because he cares for you.

Another difficulty people have is the incompetence (or perceived incompetence) of the authority figure in charge. A person has greater abilities, so they think they don't need to submit to the one placed over them. People also may squirm if the person above them is not worthy of respect or is overtly evil. The character of the person in charge is not *why* to submit to them.

For example, God didn't tell wives to yield to their husbands based on their husbands' competence or character. He was after something much greater, much deeper—in the woman, for her destiny, and as an analogy of the Bride of the Lamb. He is watching and testing—will they submit *in view of me??* Or will the potential Bride stay stiff and disqualify herself for the co-reign of the Lamb?

The other test is when any authority—a parent, a husband, a leader, a government, a teacher, etc.—directs *against* the will of God. Some will willfully comply. This shows they were yielding, not for God, but in the fear of man. We are to obey leaders "in the Lord" (see Colossians 3:18, Ephesians 6:1)

Another reason many will not submit is pride. I am "equal." Yes, but you have different strengths and responsibilities, for different reasons.

Still another reason is a fear of losing control, of losing oneself, of losing one's plans. But the truth is, your greatest protection is not from yourself but through trust in God, by obeying him. Your plans will actually be established supernaturally, by God, when you trust him to bring them about in your life, and "loosen your grip on the wheel." They happen by faith and trust. You alone will not even be able to defend yourself. Yielding when you disagree, because it's the will of God, allows God to step in and exalt.

Those who have been abused by authority can find a part of their soul sectioned off in self-protection, and find it very difficult to yield at times. But the spirit in you was not abused. The real you went unharmed. What you need is the flashlight of the Word to shine into the hurt area by the Spirit, so that you understand what happened to you and why, and get the enemy in the darkness of that area, out. Then you will realize perfectly that you can trust your loving and powerful, heavenly Father. Finding the answers will heal the soul, and yielding even when extremely uncomfortable will give you huge wings to fly.

[John 12:24-25, 27-28 E.S.V.] 24 Truly, truly, I say to you, unless a grain of wheat falls into the earth and dies, it remains alone; but if it dies, it bears much fruit. 25 Whoever [likes] his [soul] [kills] it, and whoever hates his [soul] in this world will [guard] it [unto] eternal life. ... 27 "Now is my soul troubled. And what shall I say? 'Father, save me from this hour'? But for this purpose I have come to this hour. 28 Father, glorify your name"….

The Bride compatible to the Lamb learns to yield, to maintain submissiveness, and to receive the resulting exaltation that comes from God only. She is not like Vashti, but like Queen Esther: meticulously submissive, humble, exalted and powerful through God and the help he always sends her.

Chapter 2

The Bride is Taken Out from the Body

[Matthew 13:24-30 E.S.V.] 24 He put another parable before them, saying, "The kingdom of heaven may be compared to a man who sowed good seed in his field, 25 but while his men were sleeping, his enemy came and sowed weeds among the wheat and went away. 26 So when the plants came up and bore grain, then the weeds appeared also. 27 And the servants of the master of the house came and said to him, 'Master, did you not sow good seed in your field? How then does it have weeds?' 28 He said to them, 'An enemy has done this.' So the servants said to him, 'Then do you want us to go and gather them?' 29 But he said, 'No, lest in gathering the weeds you root up the wheat along with them. 30 Let both grow together until the harvest, and at harvest time I will tell the reapers, "Gather the weeds first and bind them in bundles to be burned, but gather the wheat into my barn."'"

The "tares" look almost identical to the wheat at first and as they grow next to each other. But in the end, once they each reach maturity, the wheat bows down, and the tares stick straight up—they *cannot* bow.

Not all who are in the Body of the Chosen King, brought in through the new birth by grace, will be fit and suitable to rule with Jesus as his Bride.

[Matthew 13:47-50 NKJV] 47 "Again, the kingdom of heaven is like a dragnet that was cast into the sea and gathered some of every kind, 48 "which, when it was full, they drew to shore; and they sat down and gathered the good into vessels, but threw the bad away. 49 "So it will be at the end of the age. The angels will come forth, separate the wicked from among the just, 50 "and

cast them into the furnace of fire. There will be wailing and gnashing of teeth."

What I am sharing now will only even be understood by the Bride. It is a "great mystery."

[Ephesians 5:25-32 N.A.S.B.] 25 Husbands, love your wives, just as [The Anointed King] also loved the [Legislature] and gave Himself up for her, 26 so that He might sanctify her, having cleansed her by the washing of water with the word, 27 that He might present to Himself the [Legislature] in all her glory, having no spot or wrinkle or any such thing; but that she would be holy and blameless. 28 So husbands also ought to love their own wives as their own bodies. He who loves his own wife loves himself; 29 for no one ever hated his own flesh, but nourishes and cherishes it, just as [The Anointed King] also [does] the [Legislature], 30 because we are parts of His body. 31 FOR THIS REASON A MAN SHALL LEAVE HIS FATHER AND HIS MOTHER AND BE JOINED TO HIS WIFE, AND THE TWO SHALL BECOME ONE FLESH. 32 This mystery is great; but I am speaking with reference to [The Anointed King] and the [Legislature].

[Genesis 2:20-24 NKJV] 20 So Adam gave names to all cattle, to the birds of the air, and to every beast of the field. But for Adam there was not found a helper comparable to him. 21 And the LORD God caused a deep sleep to fall on Adam, and he slept; and He took one of his ribs, and closed up the flesh in its place. 22 Then the rib which the LORD God had taken from man He made into a woman, and He brought her to the man. 23 And Adam said: "This [is] now bone of my bones and flesh of my flesh; She shall be called Woman, because she was taken out of Man." 24 Therefore a man shall leave his father and mother and be joined to his wife, and they shall become one flesh.

The Bride comes *out* of the Body, just as Eve came out of Adam's body while he slept. During this time period, between King Jesus's first and second coming, it is like he is in a deep sleep which Adam's sleep typified. And God is in the process this whole time of shaping the Bride-to-be that he takes from the Body, into the glorious One that he will present to his Son.

[Colossians 3:1-4 N.A.S.B.] 1 Therefore if you have been raised up with [The Anointed King], keep seeking the things above, where [The Anointed King] is, seated [that is, enthroned] at the right hand of God. 2 Set your mind on the things above, not on the things that are on earth. 3 For you have died and your life is hidden with [The Anointed King] in God. 4 When [The Anointed King], who is our life, is revealed, then you also will be revealed with Him in glory.

Just as Eve was hidden inside of Adam for a time before being brought out and displayed to all of creation, the Bride is hidden at this time, in the Secret Place, in The Anointed King, in God. She is being revealed also, at the same time the Chosen King is revealed—because she is of his exact substance and nature, and in him. And this unfolding revelation is progressive, from glory to glory, until finally she looks exactly like him in glory, with no shadow on any side, and she will be "brought to the Man" (Genesis 2:22)—in Her case, the New Man.

Now is the time of development. It's the time of the removal of warts, spots and blemishes of the world, still found on her countenance because of the way she wrongly sees herself. Through the Word she is being cleansed, and by its light she is undergoing laser-surgical, beautification treatments continually.

[Hebrews 4:12-13 N.A.S.B.] 12 For the word of God is living and active and sharper than any two-edged sword, and piercing as far as the division of soul and spirit, of both joints and marrow, and able to judge the thoughts and intentions of the heart. 13 And there is no creature hidden from His sight, but all things are open and laid bare to the eyes of Him with whom we have to do.

This surgery is *thorough*. No part will be left out. As dark areas are illumined, by the fire, the deceptions/defects are burned up by that fire. The process is relentless. It is as relentless as the blue fire in the King's eyes, not satisfied till it has consumed all stubble—all that is common and not precious in Her—all corruption.

What defines the Bride is the choice to be continually tested in this fire of refinement, to subject herself to all "12 months" of the beauty treatment, till the Spirit deems her completely suitable to be brought before the King. She will be brought in wearing fully prepared, white robes.

[Revelation 19:7 N.A.S.B.] 7 "Let us rejoice and be glad and give the glory to Him, for the marriage of the Lamb has come and His bride has made herself ready."

Chapter 3

How She Learns Her Identity

Just as by natural birth, in The Anointed King we also begin with no self-awareness. But immediately, in the light of the Spirit, we begin to see what we are, by the Word. Jesus Himself is the Living Word. As we see him, who we are in, we see ourself *in him.*

[Psalm 36:9 NKJV] 9 For with You is the fountain of life; in Your light we see light.

[Revelation 19:13 NKJV] 13 ...and His name is called The Word of God.

[1 John 3:2 NKJV] 2 Beloved, now we are children of God; and it has not yet been revealed what we shall be, but we know that when He is revealed, we shall be like Him, for we shall see Him as He is.

It is amazing to realize that none of us have ever seen our own eyes. We've barely ever seen our nose. We've never seen our ears, chin, etc. To get to know those details, we need a tool. We need a mirror, and we need light. With these things provided, no one can tell us we look different than we actually look.

God has provided, for the Bride of the Lamb, a mirror: the Word of God.

[James 1:21-25 E.S.V.] 21 ...receive with meekness the implanted word, which is able to save your souls. 22 But be doers of the word, and not hearers only, deceiving yourselves. 23 For if anyone is a hearer of the word and not a doer, he is like a man

who looks intently at his natural face in a mirror. 24 For he looks at himself and goes away and at once forgets what he was like. 25 But the one who looks into the perfect law, the law of liberty…

We may have wrinkles in our face, deep ones. But we see the glory of the Lord in that mirror, which is the real us. We find out that we are His glory, that we shine actually. As he shines, we do too. It's just like a physical mirror: as you move your arm, the image you see in the mirror does too—exactly. There is a correspondence between us and the Lord that we see as we look into that mirror.

There is an enemy to this beautifying, glory-transfer process. The evil one comes near, appearing very innocent and non-aggressive. He won't even look the Bride in the eye but appears so docile. He comes with what seems like innocent entertainment, harmless enough for even a child to enjoy. He seeks attention. He seeks to get the Bride to break her gaze off of the mirror of the Word—where she sees the Lord and her glory—and onto him, as the serpent did to Eve.

That serpent appears small, skinny, like not a problem. But it encourages "over desire," of the body or the eyes. Its fangs are another mirror, but a counterfeit one that produces a *distorted* image of the woman to her. In it she sees herself in darkness, when she's really "light in the Lord." The venom of those fangs with their distorted picture is enough to make the woman lose her ability to stand, and bring her to the ground, as powerful as she is.

We need to see ourselves in the fire-light of the eyes of the Lord toward us. That light removes for us the darkness we were hiding in. In the light, we are illuminated. The light shines so brightly that we lose sight of ourself and become "naked and unashamed" again.

[1 John 1:5-9 N.A.S.B.] 5 This is the message we have heard from Him and announce to you, that God is Light, and in Him there is no darkness at all. 6 If we say that we have fellowship with Him and [yet] walk in the darkness, we lie and do not practice the truth; 7 but if we walk in the Light as He Himself is in the Light, we have fellowship with one another, and the blood of Jesus His Son cleanses us from all sin. 8 If we say that we have no sin [when we really do], we are deceiving ourselves and the truth is not in us. 9 If we confess our sins, He is faithful and righteous, so that He will forgive us our sins and cleanse us from all unrighteousness.

[Psalm 36:9 NKJV] 9 …in Your light we see light.

The fire-light burns our bonds off. The Truth sets free. It becomes a high, high wall for us of protection.

Moses built the Tabernacle in the desert, on Israel's journey to the promised land. This was basically a mobile-Temple illustration for us today, as we are the actual Temple of God. The first thing in it was the alter where the sacrifice was made, showing that it is impossible to come to God without the sacrifice of Jesus—the cross. That alter also represents *our* cross, as we lay down our lives completely for him in view of his compassion for us. This is the beginning of our progress.

[Romans 12:1-2 E.S.V.] 1 I appeal to you therefore, brothers, by the mercies of God, to present your bodies as a living sacrifice, [distinctive] and acceptable to God, which is your [reasonable] worship. 2 Do not be conformed to this world, but be transformed by the renewal of your mind, that by testing you may discern what is the will of God, what is good and acceptable and perfect [or "complete"].

Without this full commitment, which is characteristic of the Bride, there would be no progress. Nothing else of God could be accessed and enjoyed. But the Bride comes to the next element in the Tabernacle: the "brazen laver" (or, "brass washbasin").

During its construction, the women who assembled at the Tabernacle became a picture of the Bride of the Lamb when they gave their hand-mirrors—at that time made of brass—for the construction of the washbasin.

[Exodus 38:8 NKJV] 8 He made the laver of bronze and its base of bronze, from the bronze mirrors of the serving women who assembled at the door of the tabernacle of meeting.

After the alter, the priests going into the Temple would stop at the brass washbasin and cleanse themselves using two things: the mirror image they could see in the brass and the water the basin held.

[Ephesians 5:25-26 KJV] 25 …[The Anointed King]…loved the [Legislature], and gave himself for it; 26 that he might [make it distinct] and cleanse it with the washing of water by the word

The brass washbasin represents the opportunity to see ourselves in the mirror of the Word and cleanse ourselves accordingly in the water of the Word. To have it required those women give up their hand-mirrors—their ability to see themselves with *their own* mirrors.

So in order to see our image correctly, we must let go of human opinions about ourselves, or anything contrary to what the Word says about us, and look fully into the Word of God to see our image *there.* In that mirror of the Word, the water of the Word is provided, so we can splash our faces and cleanse ourselves of anything contrary to that image.

We see ourselves as we really are, and adjust to that (see 1 Corinthians 5:7). As we look into that basin, we are seeing His image in the Word, and thereby our own. He is the Truth (see John 14:6). What does He look like?

Chapter 4

She Becomes Radiant

The Bride of the Lamb becomes Radiant.

[Ephesians 5:25-27 NKJV, literal added] 25 Husbands, love your wives, just as [The Anointed King] also loved the [Legislature] and gave Himself for [it], 26 that He might sanctify and cleanse [it] with the washing of water by the word, 27 that He might present [it] to Himself a glorious [Legislature], not having spot or wrinkle or any such thing, but that [it] should be holy and without blemish.

Three of Jesus' 12 disciples went up a mountain with him one day and "saw him in his majesty" and glory (2 Peter 1:16-18):

[Matthew 17:2 NKJV] 2 and He was transfigured before them. His face shone like the sun, and His clothes became as white as the light.

[Luke 9:29 NKJV] 29 As He prayed, the appearance of His face was altered, and His robe [became] white [and] glistening.

[Mark 9:2-3 NKJV] 2 Now after six days Jesus took Peter, James, and John, and led them up on a high mountain apart by themselves; and He was transfigured before them. 3 His clothes became shining, exceedingly white, like snow, such as no launderer on earth can whiten them.

What happens now when we look at him, in the mirror of the Word? Immediately there is a transfer of his glory, from his face to ours. Just as it is recorded,

[Psalm 34:5 NKJV] 5 They looked to Him and were radiant, and their faces were not ashamed.

This "transfiguration" or "transformation" is immediate, as we look into the mirror-basin of the Word and wash ourselves with it. We become like him. It is an immense, amazing and thorough transformation that eventually changes our whole lives, which we wholly lay down before him as a lamb-sacrifice on the alter.

This "becoming" is a continual process that goes all the way to the end of our growth period on earth. And in the end:

[1 John 3:2 NKJV] 2 ...but we know that when He is revealed, we shall be like Him, for we shall see Him as He is.

[Matthew 13:43 NKJV] 43 "Then the righteous will shine forth as the sun in the kingdom of their Father. He who has ears to hear, let him hear!

This is what we endure to the end for. It's for that bridal gaze into the eyes of our Beloved—that full view of Him, as he is, when instantly the final work of transformation will be completed in us.

Those who do not set their focus on Him and endure in doing so to the end would miss this. Instead, the brightness of his light would cause them to "shrink back":

[1 John 2:28 NASB] 28 Now, little children, abide in Him, so that when He appears, we may have confidence and not shrink away from Him in shame at His coming.

[Hebrews 10:36-39 NKJV] 36 For you have need of endurance, so that after you have done the will of God, you may receive the promise: 37 "For yet a little while, [And] He who is coming will come and will not tarry. 38 Now the just shall live by faith; But if [anyone] draws back, My soul has no pleasure in him." 39 But we are not of those who draw back to perdition, but of those who believe to the saving of the soul.

It is important to *know* what you are enduring for. It is to be able to stand before him confidently and look fully into his eyes, and see you, and you will be changed. Your soul will receive the final transfiguration, "and we will be like him."

[Luke 21:34-36 N.A.S.B.] 34 "Be on guard, so that your hearts will not be weighted down with [regret for foolishness] and drunkenness and the worries of life, and that day will not come on you suddenly like a trap; 35 for it will come upon all those who dwell on the face of all the earth. 36 "But keep on the alert at all times, praying that you may have strength to escape all these things that are about to take place, and to stand before the Son of Man."

Seeing King Jesus in his glory has been terrifying. When the three disciples on the mountain saw him, they were "terrified" (Mark 9:6). John also, when he saw him in Heaven, described,

[Revelation 1:16-17 E.S.V.] 16 In his right hand he held seven stars, from his mouth came a sharp two-edged sword, and his face was like the sun shining in full strength. 17 When I saw him, I fell at his feet as though dead. But he laid his right hand on me, saying, "Fear not, I am the first and the last

The only thing that will make us stand before him on that Day is Love, brought to maturity in us. And that happens as we keep our eyes on Him, by the Truth.

[1 John 4:16-19 E.S.V.] 16 So we have come to know and to believe the love that God has for us. God is love, and whoever abides in love abides in God, and God abides in him. 17 By this is love perfected [or "made complete"] with us, so that we may have confidence for the day of judgment, because as he is so also are we in this world. 18 There is no fear in love, but [completed] love casts out fear. For fear has to do with punishment, and whoever fears has not been [completed] in love. 19 We love because he first loved us.

The more we see Love—who He is—we are conformed to the same image, as we actually are also. It becomes evident to the world that we are Love. We shine as it. It is our greatest glory.

Chapter 5

She Prepares Herself with Glory

[Revelation 19:7 N.I.V.] 7 …For the wedding of the Lamb has come, and his bride has made herself ready.

One characteristic of the Bride is her preparation for the wedding. She anticipates it and prepares herself. How? What does she use? She uses what any woman preparing herself would use, Her Mirror.

[2 Corinthians 3:17-18 N.A.S.B.] 17 Now the Lord is the Spirit, and where the Spirit of the Lord is, [there] is freedom. 18 But we all, with unveiled faces, looking as in a mirror[2] at the glory of the Lord, are being transformed into the same image from glory to glory, just as from the Lord, the Spirit.

It is the image that she "looks intently at" in the mirror of the Word? The glory of the Lord that she sees, that reveals that same glory in her, to her.

She "cannot get enough" of Him. She is continually gazing at him, to see his glory, which is hers also. She must see more of his glory. And as she looks into that mirror, she is *continually* changed.

She never has any desire to "arrive"—not until that Day. She "leaves the dock" but never arrives. She "finds him" but can never get enough of him. Her interest is in "becoming." She is preparing Herself for Him. Her glory is always increasing, as she is always looking. She is

---

2 KJV translates this "glass." All other versions translate it "mirror," and the same word is used in James 1:23 where a mirror is clearly depicted. The KJV erroneously translated "mirror" as glass here, which is a separate Greek word (Strongs Concordance).

preparing herself with glory.

There are earthly traps that seek to hold her down from the ascension of becoming, which is hers in Him. But by her persistent gazing, and the resultant glory transfer that transforms her, she eventually escapes them all. She grows huge as a disciple, a student who "continues in" Jesus' Word" (John 8:31).

We don't escape any earthly attachment by looking at the problem. But by looking at the glory of the Lord, we are transformed.

[Psalm 25:15 N.A.S.B.] 15 My eyes are continually toward the LORD, For He will rescue my feet from the net.

The Bride's heart is set on pilgrimage, on "becoming."

[Psalm 84:5-7 N.I.V.] 5 Blessed are those whose strength is in you, whose hearts are set on pilgrimage. 6 As they pass through the Valley of Baka, they make it a place of springs; the autumn rains also cover it with pools. 7 They go from strength to strength, till each appears before God in Zion.

There is an earthly Zion: Jerusalem, "the city of the great King." It has always been special, and the Lord will eventually be welcomed from there, in fulfilment of ancient prophecies (for example, "Luke 13:35). But there is also a "Jerusalem that is above" (Galatians 4:26), the "new Jerusalem" that comes out of God, "prepared like a bride adorned for husband" (Revelation 21:2). The Bride of the Lamb is set on pilgrimage till she appears in and as a part of *that city*.

The Bride will *only be satisfied* with the Bridegroom, with seeing him in all of his radiant glory, gazing face-to-face. She will only be satisfied with removing her wedding veil at that time to look him directly in the eyes. She is content *only* with the process of metamorphosis, until that day. Nothing else will satisfy her—no achievement, no human prize or accolades, no knowledge.

[Psalm 17:15 E.S.V.] 15 As for me, I shall behold your face in righteousness; when I awake, I shall be satisfied with your likeness.

She wants her Bridegroom!

[Song of Songs, 3:1-4 E.S.V.] 1 ...I sought him whom my soul loves; I sought him, but found him not. 2 I will rise now and go about the city, in the streets and in the squares; I will seek him whom my soul loves. I sought him, but found him not. 3 The watchmen found me as they went about in the city. "Have you seen him whom my soul loves?" 4 Scarcely had I passed them when I found him whom my soul loves. I held him, and would not let him go until I had brought him into my mother's house, and into the chamber of her who conceived me.

I mentioned that her heart is *set* on pilgrimage. Abraham is a father of those who walk by faith (see Romans 4:12). His beginning with God was like this:

[Genesis 12:1-2 N.A.S.B.] 1 Now the LORD said to Abram, "Go from your country, and from your relatives and from your father's house, to the land which I will show you; 2 and I will make you into a great nation, and I will bless you, and make your name great; and [you shall] be a blessing

In his journey, Abraham was always in search of something beyond the physical:

[Hebrews 11:8-10 E.S.V.] 8 By faith Abraham obeyed when he was called to go out to a place that he was to receive as an inheritance. And he went out, not knowing where he was going. 9 By faith he went to live in the land of promise, as in a foreign land, living in tents with Isaac and Jacob, heirs with him of the same promise. 10 For he was looking forward to the city that has foundations, whose designer and builder is God.

He wanted the City. He detached from the physical for it, as did others:

[Hebrews 11:13b-16 E.S.V.] 13 ...not having received the things promised, but having seen them and greeted them from afar, and having acknowledged that they were strangers and exiles on the earth. 14 For people who speak thus make it clear that they are seeking a homeland. 15 If they had been thinking of that land from which they had gone out, they would have had opportunity

to return. 16 But as it is, they desire a better country, that is, a heavenly one. Therefore God is not ashamed to be called their God, for he has prepared for them a city.

The Bride today is the same. The Bridegroom continually calls her to himself:

[Song of Songs 2:10 E.S.V.] 10 My beloved speaks and says to me: "Arise, my love, my beautiful one, and come away

Psalm 45 contains an illustration of the Chosen King and his Queen. In one part there is an exhortation to God's daughter now, in preparation for the Wedding:

[Psalm 45:10-11 E.S.V.] 10 Hear, O daughter, and consider, and incline your ear: forget your people and your father's house, 11 and the king will desire your beauty. Since he is your lord, bow to him.

Where does the Bride go from glory to glory? She is placed in the midst of darkness and given access to the knowledge of God, which shines with the glory of the Lord. It is found in "the ordinary," a treasure placed in earthen vessels. She has to dig for it, as for a treasure in a field. By giving her all, she obtains access to it, and by seeking, she will find it. The glory of that treasure shines so thickly, so immensely, that it's worth all of the seeking. She sees her own image in it—her face is transfigured by that knowledge—her true beauty and glory is then found and can be seen. These are like clay, beauty treatments, applied continually.

There is a light that is to be streaming to us continually:

[2 Corinthians 4:6-7 N.A.S.B.] 6 For God, who said, "Light shall shine out of darkness," is the One who has shone in our hearts to give the Light of the knowledge of the glory of God in the face of [The Anointed King]. 7 But we have this treasure in earthen [or, physical] vessels, so that the surpassing greatness of the power will be of God and not from ourselves

This is how the Bride lightens the darkness. She continually refers to the picture—the image found in the Mirror, the glory of the Lord she bows to. And she is continually refreshed by the river she kneels down by.

She is constantly looking. She won't stop beholding. The darkness cannot distract her. Her renewing by the Image and transformation to it is too important for her. So she keeps transforming and shining brighter and brighter, in the midst of darkness. She is the Light.

[2 Corinthians 4:16-18 N.A.S.B.] 16 Therefore we do not lose heart, but though our outer man is decaying, yet our inner man is being renewed day by day. 17 For momentary, light affliction is producing for us an eternal weight of glory far beyond all comparison, 18 while we look not at the things which are seen, but at the things which are not seen; for the things which are seen are temporal, but the things which are not seen are eternal.

[Philippians 2:15 NKJV] 15 ...children of God without fault in the midst of a crooked and perverse generation, among whom you shine as lights [or "luminaries," or "stars"] in the world

[Matthew 5:14 NKJV] 14 "You are the light of the world.

The Bride's beginning does not matter. She goes continually from glory to glory as she sees herself, by "x-ray vision," inside of The Anointed King. As she acts on what she sees, she is continually transformed to the same Image to display the exact same glory, for those on the earth.

The water she uses to wash her face with is the glory of the Lord. The Spirit shows His image to her in the Word, and this results in her glory.

[Ephesians 5:25-27 KJV] 25 ...[The Anointed King] also loved the [Legislature], and gave himself for it; 26 that he might sanctify [that is, "set it apart"] and cleanse it with the washing of water by the word, 27 That he might present it to himself a glorious [Legislature], not having spot, or wrinkle, or any such thing; but that it should be holy [that is, "distinctive"] and without blemish.

Chapter 6

Her Self-Denial, Pleasure & Service

To see the Bride, you have to see the The Anointed King because she is in Him and continually conforming to his image. The Christ means literally, the Anointed King, which means the one chosen and appointed and empowered by God to rule. He rules, he reigns, he is dominant and above all, the strongest, the richest, the most powerful and glorious and brightest. The Jewish People of God in Jesus' day had that picture in mind and they were waiting for him to appear and deliver them from their physical oppressors.

They didn't take note of the other half of his image: the suffering servant, the "lamb upon the throne, looking as if it had been slain" (see Revelation 5:6). He's not only the Lion but also, at the same time, the Lamb. And he is portraying, exactly, the image of the Father. He is "a priest upon the throne" (Zechariah 6:13). As a priest, he sacrificed Himself, out of pure love for us. And he has invited us to be and do the same (see Revelation 1:5, 1 John 3:16).

I was learning a new language some years back, and as a kind of textbook I was using Matthew, Mark, Luke and John. So for a long time, daily, I read through these books over and over and over. As I did so I began to notice some patterns. I noticed how often Jesus publicly spoke about the Kingdom. I also noticed that the statement repeated the most in the Gospels was Jesus telling his inner circle that he would suffer and be crucified in Jerusalem. For example:

[Matthew 16:21 NKJV] 21 From that time Jesus began to show to His disciples that He must go to Jerusalem, and suffer many things from the elders and chief priests and scribes, and be killed, and be raised the third day.

[Matthew 20:17-19 NKJV] 17 Now Jesus, going up to Jerusalem, took the twelve disciples aside on the road and said to them, 18 "Behold, we are going up to Jerusalem, and the Son of Man will be betrayed to the chief priests and to the scribes; and they will condemn Him to death, 19 "and deliver Him to the Gentiles to mock and to scourge and to crucify. And the third day He will rise again."

The second most frequent statement he made was that his followers must also take up and endure *their* cross and follow him to be his disciple:

[Matthew 10:38-39 NKJV, literal added] 38 "And he who does not take his cross and follow after Me is not worthy of Me. 39 "He who finds his [soul] will [kill] it, and he who [kills] his [soul] for My sake will find it.

[Luke 9:21-26 NKJV, literal added] 21 And He strictly warned and commanded them to tell this to no one, 22 saying, "The Son of Man must suffer many things, and be rejected by the elders and chief priests and scribes, and be killed, and be raised the third day." 23 Then He said to [them] all, "If anyone desires to come after Me, let him deny himself, and take up his cross daily, and follow Me. 24 "For whoever desires to save his [soul] will [kill] it, but whoever [kills] his [soul] for My sake will save it. 25 "For what profit is it to a man if he gains the whole world, and is himself [killed] or [suffers loss]? 26 "For whoever is ashamed of Me and My words, of him the Son of Man will be ashamed when He comes in His [own] glory, and [in His] Father's, and of the holy angels.

His cross is always first. "We love because he first loved us" (1 John 4:19). It is "in view of the mercy of God" that we "offer our bodies as living sacrifices…our logical act of worship" (Romans 12:1). Whenever God's People lose sight of the cross, their pure devotion begins to diminish (see Galatians 3:1). Also, they start giving way to earthly law, which is the power of sin, to try to serve or become righteous by. They get off the foundation of God's grace in The Anointed King (see Galatians, Romans 7, Romans 12:1-2, 1 Corinthians 15:56-57). But in view of the cross, we can worship fully.

Taking up our cross is the voluntary choice to do God's will over our own, to "deny self," otherwise known as "killing the soul." In these verses, the actual meaning of the word, "life" is "soul," and the meaning of "lose" is "kill" (or "put to death"):

[Matthew 16:21-27 NKJV, literal added] 21 From that time Jesus began to show to His disciples that He must go to Jerusalem, and suffer many things from the elders and chief priests and scribes, and be killed, and be raised the third day. 22 Then Peter took Him aside and began to rebuke Him, saying, "Far be it from You, Lord; this shall not happen to You!" 23 But He turned and said to Peter, "Get behind Me, Satan! You are an offense to Me, for you are not mindful of the things of God, but the things of men." 24 Then Jesus said to His disciples, "If anyone desires to come after Me, let him deny himself, and take up his cross, and follow Me. 25 "For whoever desires to save his [soul] will [kill] it, but whoever [kills] his [soul] for My sake will find it. 26 "For what profit is it to a man if he gains the whole world, and [suffer loss] [regarding his] soul? Or what will a man give in exchange for his soul [that is, to get his soul back]? 27 "For the Son of Man will come in the glory of His Father with His angels, and then He will reward each according to his works.

[Mark 8:34-38 NKJV, literal added] 34 When He had called the people to [Himself], with His disciples also, He said to them, "Whoever desires to come after Me, let him deny himself, and take up his cross, and follow Me. 35 "For whoever desires to save his [soul] will [kill] it, but whoever [kills] his [soul] for My sake and the gospel's will save it. 36 "For what will it profit a man if he gains the whole world, and [suffer loss] [regarding his] soul? 37 "Or what will a man give in exchange for his soul? 38 "For whoever is ashamed of Me and My words in this adulterous and sinful generation, of him the Son of Man also will be ashamed when He comes in the glory of His Father with the holy angels."

The soul of a person is one of three parts, and it is in the process of being saved (see James 1:21, 1 Peter 1:22, Hebrews 10:39). The Spirit is far, far greater and bigger, and the predominant part of what we are (see John 3:6, Hebrews 12:9). The soul is a small part of us, on the inside. As we identify with our spirit and walk by the Truth, it sometimes opposes our forward progress, with desires contrary to God's will. The Good News is, when it does so you can put it to death. This is what it means to "deny yourself, take up your cross and follow me."

As our Leader, Jesus exemplified this for us:

[John 12:23-28 NKJV, literal added] 23 But Jesus answered them, saying, "The hour has come that the Son of Man should be glorified. 24 "Most assuredly, I say to you, unless a grain of wheat falls into the ground and dies, it remains alone; but if it dies, it produces much grain. 25 "He who [likes] his [soul] will [kill] it, and he who hates his [soul] in this world will [protect] it for eternal life. 26 "If anyone serves Me, let him follow Me; and where I am, there My servant will be also. If anyone serves Me, him [My] Father will honor. 27 "Now My soul is troubled, and what shall I say? 'Father, save Me from this hour'? But for this purpose I came to this hour. 28 "Father, glorify Your name." Then a voice came from heaven, [saying], "I have both glorified [it] and will glorify [it] again."

[Matthew 26:36-39 NKJV] 36 Then Jesus came with them to a place called Gethsemane, and said to the disciples, "Sit here while I go and pray over there." 37 And He took with Him Peter and the two sons of Zebedee, and He began to be sorrowful and deeply distressed. 38 Then He said to them, "My soul is exceedingly sorrowful, even to death. Stay here and watch with Me." 39 He went a little farther and fell on His face, and prayed, saying, "O My Father, if it is possible, let this cup pass from Me; nevertheless, not as I will, but as You [will]."

The beautification process of the Bride includes the two treatments, illustrated by Esther's preparation to be queen:

[Esther 2:12 N.A.S.B.] 12 ...twelve months under the regulations for the women for the days of their beautification...as follows: six months with oil of myrrh and six months with spices and the cosmetics for women

The sufferings that are "according to the will of God" (1 Peter 4:19) and "appointed for us" (1 Thessalonians 3:3) are to allow the

Bride to be "conformed to [the image of] Jesus' death" (Philippians 3:10). And these beauty treatments are never wasted but only "if necessary." They serve to refine our faith, for a permanent and eternal benefit (see 1 Peter 1:6-7). They are indelible, invaluable, irreplaceable, and inestimable.

This kind of suffering is *not* random, not accidental, nor unmanaged. It is not "beyond what we are able" to endure through God's grace and strength (see 1 Corinthians 10:13). It is not stemming from ignorance or foolishness.

These *look* bad to the human eye, like the mud beauty treatments that women sometimes voluntarily undergo. But they are so healthy for the Bride—so full of beauty enhancing minerals and enrichments. They are only for a time and as necessary. They are our Father's training, and though this training is painful, in the end it yields the "peaceable fruit of righteousness for those who allow themselves to be trained fully by it" (see Hebrews 12:11).

So the Bride, who learns to yield, in the process saves her soul. By denying herself, for the will of God, she is beautified and prepared to reign with King Jesus.

The Bride also undergoes glorious beauty treatments of exquisite pleasure. God's warm, strong light shines on her, so that she experiences all pleasantness in life. There is no end to the pleasure she enjoys in Him.

[Psalm 16:11 E.S.V.] 11 You make known to me the path of life; in your presence there is fullness of joy; at your right hand are pleasures forevermore.

[1 Timothy 6:17 NKJV] 17 ...God...gives us richly all things to enjoy.

[Isaiah 1:19 NKJV] 19 If you are willing and obedient, you shall eat the good of the land

Like Esther, the Bride departs from any low-level thinking; she gets used to the palace, to royal treatment. She is secure in God's high tower of exaltation. She is trained to not think low of herself, only highly of herself. She is royalty, she shines increasingly, and she knows it. This aspect of what she sees in the mirror of the Word is so important. She knows she is being "invited and summoned to his own

Kingdom and glory." Therefore, she can "walk in a manner worthy of it" (see 1 Thessalonians 2:12).

She learns that she is "in The Anointed King," that she is exalted beyond measure, enthroned with him and sharing his glory and Kingdom reign (see Ephesians 1-3; 2 Corinthians 12:7, NKJV; Romans 8:29-30). She knows that "no good thing will God withhold from those whose walk is blameless" (Psalm 84:11), and that this especially includes her. She learns that she is "highly favored in the Beloved" (see Matthew 3:17, 12:18, Ephesians 1:6). She learns she has been given "all things that pertain to life and godliness" (2 Peter 1:3), and that she *possesses all things*! (see John 17:10, 1 Corinthians 3:22, 2 Corinthians 6:10). And these include:

[James 1:17-18 NKJV] 17 Every good gift and every perfect gift is from above, and comes down from the Father of lights, with whom there is no variation or shadow of turning. 18 Of His own will He brought us forth by the word of truth, that we might be a kind of firstfruits of His creatures.

As she cooperates with the preparation process, she knows that no good thing will be withheld from her. For example:

[Proverbs 24:3-4 NKJV] 3 Through wisdom a house is built, And by understanding it is established; 4 By knowledge the rooms are filled With all precious and pleasant riches.

The Bride prospers in every way. She extends her branches in all directions, to flourish and bear fruit. Like Jesus while on earth, she learns how to make and manage money supernaturally. Jesus had a treasurer on earth and, rather than being poor, he gave to the poor. She also "extends her hand to the poor, and she stretches out her hands to the needy" (Proverbs 31:20).

Extending out her hands represents help. She doesn't indefinitely give money to the poor—no. She rescues them out of poverty, with a helping hand. Of course, this is King Jesus' way also. They both serve to dignify the one trapped in poverty, to bring them out of it.

Every area of her life and dealings prospers, even amid adversity (see Mark 10:29-30).

[3 John verse 2 NKJV] 2 Beloved, I pray that you may prosper in

all things and be in health, just as your soul prospers.

And most importantly to her, as it was written about her King, "the good pleasure of the LORD will prosper in his hand" (Isaiah 53:10), so God's good pleasure will prosper in her hand also.

The Bride's main desire is to please her Lord. Regardless of what season she is in, or what she is experiencing, her highest motivations are to know him and to please him.

[Colossians 1:10 NKJV] 10 that you may walk worthy of the Lord, fully pleasing [Him], being fruitful in every good work and increasing in the knowledge of God

As Jesus said,

[John 8:28-29 NKJV] 28 Then Jesus said to them, "When you lift up the Son of Man, then you will know that I am [He], and [that] I do nothing of Myself; but as My Father taught Me, I speak these things. 29 "And He who sent Me is with Me. The Father has not left Me alone, for I always do those things that please Him."

Another aspect of the Bride is that she serves. This goes along with her ability to deny herself, because the soul of fallen man seeks to exalt itself. Human religion is always based on this. It always builds hierarchies based on human prestige, and religious spirits of pride travel up and down them and station themselves there.

That's not to say that the Kingdom does not have order, but the leadership in it serves. It's completely upside down compared to a typical business or governmental organization.

This is her way of promotion, which provides rest. She never seeks to raise herself up, but rather stoops down to serve. And GOD exalts her. Her way up is down. She is also beautified by this process.

In this way, the Bride can never be offended in life. She may feel the sting of offense, but it has no effect on her. You cannot offend a servant. You cannot hurt the lowest person. She has nowhere lower to go. She chose the lowest place, on purpose.

Why? She is destined to be seated at the highest exalted place next to the exalted King, forever. She learns, from his example and teaching, that the value of her enthronement (which came through his cross) is that she can choose to go down in order to lift others up, and this in turn lifts *Her up.* By walking out this process during our short time here, she becomes compatible with the Lamb, the crucified One. (See Philippians 2:3-11, John 13:1-17, Mark 10:40-45, Matthew 19:27-30, Luke 14:7-11).

The Bride starts out exalted, through the grace she receives, in The Anointed King. She is already exalted to the highest place, from the moment she is born from above. She is royal, enthroned with him, and begins reigning in life from the start. But to complete her responsibility of reigning, and to be effective in her reign, she stoops down and serves.

She's not a servant first but a part of the most highly exalted King. She serves in order to extend her reign to the farthest possible outpost, her shine to the farthest possible reaches. And she will be exalted as a reward for it.

Like Jesus, we are kings who serve.

Chapter 7

She Becomes Absolutely Distinctive

[Psalm 45:13 N.A.S.B.] 13 The King's daughter is all glorious within…

The greatest characteristic of the Bride is her God-like distinctiveness. She receives it as she views her Father and her Bridegroom.

[1 Peter 1:16 N.A.S.B.] 16 …"YOU SHALL BE HOLY, FOR I AM HOLY."

Better English translations of "holy" and related words would be:

- "Holy" (Greek: *hagios*) = distinct, different, set apart, separate, unlike anything else
- "Saint" (Greek: *agios*) = a distinctive one, one set apart from the rest and treasured as a special possession
- "Sanctify" (Greek: *hagiazo*) = to make distinctive, to set apart
- "Sanctification" (Greek: *hagiasmos*) = distinctiveness, or the process of making distinctive, of setting apart

God is distinctive, and he gives this same distinctiveness to His People. This was true to a degree for Israel under the Old Covenant. God said to them, "Because I am the Lord your God, you are to be distinct from all the nations of the earth, for I am distinct" (see Leviticus 20:26). This is also true for his People today, separated out from Israel and all Gentile nations, into the risen, Anointed King, to be his Legislative Body on earth. That calling itself is distinctive.

[2 Timothy 1:9 NKJV] 9 [God] has saved us and called [us] with a holy [or "distinctive"] calling, not according to our works, but according to His own purpose and grace which was given to us in [The Anointed King] Jesus before time began

The calling is distinctive, and we are called to be distinctive.

[1 Thessalonians 4:7 NKJV] 7 For God did not call us to uncleanness, but in holiness [or "sanctification": distinctiveness]

[1 Corinthians 1:2 NKJV] 2 To the [Legislature] of God which is at Corinth, to those who are [set apart] in [The Anointed King] Jesus, called [to be] [distinctive ones]...

Holy essentially means "set apart," "different," and "distinctive." The opposite of this distinctiveness is "*common*." For example,

[Ezekiel 22:26 E.S.V.] 26 Her priests have done violence to my law and have profaned my holy things. They have made no distinction between the holy and the common, neither have they taught the difference between the unclean and the clean...

We have been set apart, and we must see that we are "clothed with Christ [the Anointed King]" (Galatians 3:27); we are not ordinary *at all!!* Not at all!!!

Here are four analogies in Scripture to illustrate our distinctiveness:

The first is Joseph's coat of many colors. This unique coat made him distinct among his brothers. It set him apart from them, so much so that they saw the difference and despised and hated him. They accused him of being prideful, but really, he had not done anything wrong. He had simply been loved and favored by his father and he believed God's Word when it came to him. The Bride also experiences this kind of treatment, sometimes from spiritual siblings in the Body (see Song of Songs 5:7).

Joseph kept himself distinct through God, despite mistreatment and temptations. So at the end of his father, Israel's life when he spoke blessings and judgments on his 12 sons, He said this to Joseph:

[Genesis 49:26 NKJV] 26 The blessings of your father have excelled the blessings of my ancestors, up to the utmost bound of

the everlasting hills. They shall be on the head of Joseph, and on the crown of the head of him who was separate from his brothers.

The next analogy of distinctiveness is found in Psalm 45. This Psalm is written about God the King, Jesus the King he appointed, and his Bride. This statement refers to the Bride, God's Daughter:

[Psalm 45:13-14 N.A.S.B.] 13 The King's daughter is all glorious within; Her clothing is interwoven with gold. 14 She will be brought to the King in colorful garments...

The interweaving of gold in the Queen's clothing, is a picture of her distinctiveness.

A third analogy for our distinctiveness is salt:

[Matthew 5:13 NKJV] 13 "You are the salt of the earth; but if the salt loses its flavor, how shall it be seasoned? It is then good for nothing but to be thrown out and trampled underfoot by men.

And a fourth is light:

[Matthew 5:14-16 NKJV] 14 "You are the light of the world. A city that is set on a hill cannot be hidden. 15 "Nor do they light a lamp and put it under a basket, but on a lampstand, and it gives light to all [who are] in the house. 16 "Let your light so shine before men, that they may see your good works and glorify your Father in heaven.

God "is light, and in him is no darkness" (1 John 1:5). He is "the Father of lights, with whom there is no variation or shifting shadow" (James 1:17).

When Jesus came into the world he became "the light of the world" (see John 8:12). One thing about light is that it cannot be measured. It is used to measure things too vast for humans to measure, by "light years." Light is difficult to define, and it, itself cannot be measured.

When Jesus was born into this world as a baby, Light had come. His face shone with light. He was *different.* He came to darkness.

[Matthew 4:16 NKJV] 16 The people who sat in darkness have

seen a great light, and upon those who sat in the region and shadow of death Light has dawned."

He came to darkness. Even Mary, his mother, was darkness. Jesus said that John the baptizer was the greatest of humans, before the Kingdom of God came. But he too was darkness.

[John 1:6-9 E.S.V.] 6 There was a man sent from God, whose name was John. 7 He came as a witness, to bear witness about the light, that all might believe through him. 8 He was not the light, but came to bear witness about the light. 9 The true light, which gives light to everyone, was coming into the world.

Jesus came to enlighten all, and "those who did receive him" were authorized to be born of God, who is light and the Father of lights (John 1:12-13). Now, you have become equally unmeasurable. Jesus said himself:

[John 9:5 E.S.V.] 5 As long as I am in the world, I am the light of the world."

And about you and I, he said:

[Matthew 5:14 E.S.V.] 14 "You are the light of the world. A city set on a hill cannot be hidden.

The Body of the risen, Appointed King is of a completely different substance than those not born of God.

[Ephesians 5:8 N.A.S.B.] 8 for you were formerly darkness, but now you are Light in the Lord; walk as children of Light

The difference between the Body and those from within it who will become the Bride, is that though both are light, the Bride actually chooses to *walk* as a child of light. In other words, she chooses to shine in the midst of darkness, to not hide her light under a basket (preoccupation with work) or a bed (complacency, lack of alertness, or foolishness). She follows Jesus's footsteps to shine as light for the world. Of the Bride, this following verse is written:

[John 1:5 N.A.S.B.] 5 The Light shines in the darkness, and the darkness did not comprehend it.

The word for "comprehend" here could also be translated "take hold of, detect, understand, catch, or capture." It shines—*now*. This is describing us today. We are like the blazing bush that Moses stood before, that was a mystery to him. We are of God now.

[1 John 3:1-3 N.A.S.B., literal added] 1 See how great a love the Father has bestowed on us, that we would be called children of God; and [such] we are. For this reason the world does not know us, because it did not know Him. 2 Beloved, now we are children of God, and it has not appeared as yet what we will be. We know that when He appears, we will be like Him, because we will see Him just as He is. 3 And everyone who has this [anticipation] [resting] on Him purifies himself, just as He is pure.

We beautify ourselves, with the purifying treatment of continually seeing him as he is revealed. This is our secret facial treatment, that we apply in private, before going out into the world. It's how we prepare to display the immense glory that we have in Him.

We cannot be understood or categorized by the world, but we can shine for them. In our light rays, of the glory of God, they can see and get a slight glimpse of us momentarily.

Our Father is set apart, distinctive. His Spirit is, of course, also distinctive. And his Son Jesus is also:

[Luke 1:35 N.A.S.B.] 35 The angel answered and said to [Mary], "The Holy [or "distinctive"] Spirit will come upon you, and the power of the Most High will overshadow you; and for that reason the holy [or "distinctive"] Child shall be called the Son of God.

And his People are also.

We are distinctively set apart because we are connected to him. Everything about us was changed, including our nature, when we became his People.

[1 Peter 2:9-12 N.A.S.B.] 9 But you are A CHOSEN RACE, A royal PRIESTHOOD, A HOLY [that is, "DISTINCTIVE"] NATION, A PEOPLE FOR [God's] OWN POSSESSION, so

that you may proclaim the excellencies of Him who has called you out of darkness into His marvelous light; 10 for you once were NOT A PEOPLE, but now you are THE PEOPLE OF GOD; you had NOT RECEIVED MERCY, but now you have RECEIVED MERCY. 11 Beloved, I urge you as aliens and strangers to abstain from fleshly lusts which wage war against the soul. 12 Keep your behavior excellent among the Gentiles, so that in the thing in which they slander you as evildoers, they may because of your good deeds, as they observe [them,] glorify God in the day of visitation.

Notice it says "among the Gentiles," but he was speaking to Believers who are "Gentiles according to the flesh." So what had they become? Were they now Jews? No, no. They became a part of The New Man, called out from among both Jews and Gentiles, from every nation (see Romans 9:24-26, Revelation 5:9). That New Man is absolutely distinctive in nature.

[Galatians 6:15 NKJV] 15 For in [The Anointed King] Jesus neither circumcision [that is, being a Jew] nor uncircumcision [that is, being a Gentile] avails anything, but a new creation.

We are to first, *acknowledge* the distinctiveness we have already been given, in The Anointed King. Second, *walk according* to that image, so that we become exquisitely distinctive in every single area of our lives, every part of us becoming filled with glory, as we continually behold Him.

[1 Peter 1:14-16 NKJV, literal added] 14 as obedient children, not conforming yourselves to the former [excessive desires], [as] in your ignorance; 15 but as He who called you [is] [distinctive], you also be [distinctive] in all [your] conduct, 16 because it is written, "Be [set apart as distinct], for I am [set apart as distinct]."

There is a continual change that takes place in our character and actions, through receiving and applying the continually flowing, Word of God.

Here are seven origins of our God-like distinctiveness:

1. *The Blood-Sacrifice of Jesus*

[Revelations 1:5] "To him who loved us and freed us from our sins by his blood…"

[Hebrews 13:12 NKJV] 12 Therefore Jesus also, that He might sanctify the people [that is, "set the people apart"] with His own blood, suffered outside the gate.

We were set apart instantly by his blood, when we believed and acknowledged Jesus as Lord. There was an instant transfer of God's nature and distinctiveness to us.

We have to know and hold tightly to the fact that we were *already* made distinctive. That's the foundation we build on. We need to know it's true about us before showing it; it was given to us as a gift.

[1 Corinthians 6:11 NKJV] 11 …such were some of you. But you were washed, but you were sanctified ["set apart"], but you were justified ["made right"] in the name of the Lord Jesus and by the Spirit of our God.

2. *Our Faith (obedience of faith)*

[Revelation 1:5 NKJV] 5 and from Jesus [The Anointed King], the faithful witness, the firstborn from the dead, and the ruler over the kings of the earth. To Him who loved us and washed us from our sins in His own blood,

We are people of faith, who can see based on God's light, not just by the light used on the earth. This makes us totally different from and walking totally differently than the people in darkness, who do not know God. It was by faith that we received our distinctiveness through grace, and it is by faith that we walk with God.

Our faith is the foundation of our obedience, in the New Covenant. We have been brought to what's called, "the obedience of faith" (see Romans 1:5, 16:26). This sets us apart from the people of the world, whose attempts to do right are by outward rules and laws.

3. *Acknowledging the Righteousness We Were Given*

[Romans 5:17 E.S.V.] 17 For if, because of one man's trespass, death reigned through that one man, much more will those who receive the abundance of grace and the free gift of righteousness reign in life through the one man Jesus [The Anointed King].

We received the gift of righteousness. It was by "grace" (that is, generosity). It is real. So real that it changes the course of our whole lives, if we live according to the Truth of it.

[1 John 2:29 E.S.V.] 29 If you know that he is righteous, you may be sure that everyone who practices righteousness has been born of him.

[1 John 3:7 E.S.V.] 7 Little children, let no one deceive you. Whoever practices righteousness is righteous, as he is righteous.

[Romans 6:17-19 E.S.V., literal added] 17 But [by the grace of] God, you who were once slaves of sin have become obedient from the heart to the standard of teaching to which you were committed, 18 and, having been set free from sin, have become slaves of righteousness… so now present your members as slaves to righteousness leading to [distinctiveness].

It's by acknowledging the righteousness we now have, and therefore walking in it, that our distinctiveness shines through us into the world.

In other words we don't say, "I am a sinner…," but "I am righteous." Many Believers seem to have been influenced by the "Accuser of the Brothers," to think that they are a mixture, that they are not *really* righteous. We are truly righteous to the core of our being, being righteousness even by nature now—God's own righteousness (see 2 Corinthians 5:21). We are thoroughly and totally right, with him and by him.

"In him there is no sin" (1 John 3:5). We are in him. There is no sin in us either. "In him there is no darkness at all" (1 John 1:5). We also are "light in the Lord" now, "to walk as children of light" now.

The Bride learns to look at Herself in the Mirror and believe it, regardless of the flying arrows of wrongly intoxicated, zealously religious people. Scripture affirms over and over and over that we are now righteous. This image transfers into every area of our lives as we keep focused on it in the Mirror.

Living like this will cause the archers on the wall to shoot at you. It will cause your own Brothers & Sisters to oppose you, like Joseph's did him. But God said to do so. The Bride is singly focused on what God says, so all contrary voices, conversations and whispers fade out into nothingness.

4. Our Worship: the Offering of Our Bodies

Enabled to view God's compassion in such a way that it becomes real to her, the Bride presents her body to him on the altar "as a living sacrifice, *set apart as distinctive*, acceptable to God, which is [her] reasonable act of worship" (Romans 12:1). This is an act of consecration—the giving of one's body, including one's time, relationships, work, and everything in the body—to God. This is acceptable to God. It is the starting point. And a distinctive fire is applied to the sacrifice of her body.

And it's there that our minds have access to the supernatural knowledge of God—the Lamp that illumines—for the renewing of the mind. As the mind is renewed, the beautiful metamorphosis-transformation takes place, for a more elaborate display of distinctiveness.

Worship is to be accompanied by distinctiveness. The Bride's distinctiveness is her beauty, and God himself loves to see her worship in it.

[Psalm 29:2 NKJV] 2 Give unto the LORD the glory due to His name; worship the LORD in the beauty of holiness.

This alone is motivation enough for God's People to live a set apart life; it makes our worship glorious.

5. The Continual Cleansing of the Word

We've talked about the brass washbasin in which is found the mirror and the water. Continually applying the cleansing of the Word sets us apart as the Bride:

[Ephesians 5:25-27 N.I.V., literal added] 25 …[The Anointed King] loved the [Legislature] and gave himself up for [it] 26 to

[set it apart], cleansing [it] by the washing with water through the word, 27 and to present her to himself as a radiant church, without stain or wrinkle or any other blemish, but holy and blameless.

In Jesus prayer for us before he was crucified, he prayed:

[John 17:17 E.S.V.] 17 Sanctify them [that is, "set them apart as distinctive"] in the truth; your word is truth.

This is a supernatural, laser surgery that takes place through long-term application of the Word. It beautifies our face for completely, smooth and blemish-free skin.

6. *The Spirit of Holiness*

In all aspects of our distinctiveness, one Person is always involved: "The Spirit of Distinctiveness" (or, "the Spirit of Holiness"), who is also called, "the Spirit of Truth" (see John 14:17, 15:26, 16:13). He is not only distinct himself, but also makes distinct. He is "the Chief Eunuch" in charge of the Bride's preparation, as Hegai was to Esther. He holds the instrument of the Word and applies it to us skillfully for beautification.

[2 Corinthians 3:17-18 E.S.V.] 17 Now the Lord is the Spirit, and where the Spirit of the Lord is, there is freedom. 18 And we all, with unveiled face, beholding the glory of the Lord, are being transformed [or "transfigured"] into the same image from one degree of glory to another. For this comes from the Lord who is the Spirit.

7. The Training of Our Father

Our Father is personally involved in our process of being set apart, our "sanctification" process.

[Hebrews 12:9-10 E.S.V.] 9…we have had earthly fathers who disciplined [or "trained"] us and we respected them. Shall we not much more be subject to the Father of spirits and live? 10 For they disciplined us for a short time as it seemed best to them, but

he disciplines us for our good, that we may share his holiness.

Whether from God's training or, in some cases, his fatherly, temporary, punishment, God is giving his Children the divine opportunity to "share his distinctiveness."

There is a devotion to distinctiveness that is characteristic of the Bride. She *must* be like her Bridegroom. She is always seeking Truth, in which she can find the Image, in the Light. She will look anywhere and go through anything to find it. There is a voracious desire in her. Though she may pace herself, she has real zeal on the inside and it shapes her lifestyle.

The highest aspect of holiness is Love—it is the hottest of our flames. And by remaining in love—which is to remain in its flames—we remain blameless. The fire burns off anything not of us, so nothing from the outside can stick on us.

[1 Thessalonians 3:12-13 E.S.V.] 12 and may the Lord make you increase and abound in love for one another and for all, as we do for you, 13 so that he may establish your hearts blameless in holiness ["distinctiveness"] before our God and Father, at the coming of our Lord Jesus with all his saints [that is, "distinctive ones"].

[Philippians 1:9-11 NKJV] 9 And this I pray, that your love may abound still more and more in knowledge and all discernment, 10 that you may approve the things that are excellent, that you may be sincere and without offense till the day of [The Anointed King], 11 being filled with the fruits of righteousness which [are] by Jesus [The Anointed King], to the glory and praise of God.

When the Passover lamb was sacrificed in ancient Israel each year, it first had to be examined thoroughly and found to be without spot or blemish (Exodus 12:5). Jesus also faced examination in Jerusalem before being crucified, and he was found and declared to be blameless.

The two pressures of examination and accusation only serve to prepare the distinctive Bride for public service and display. By her continual submission to the powerful, steady, waterfall of the cleansing water of the Word, she is washed in her thinking and set apart or the Wedding. She is made spotless/blameless in love, according to the image of Jesus.

Chapter 8

The Bride's Maturity

In the last chapter, we discussed the Bride's beauty, which is her *distinctiveness*. We saw that it is a defining characteristic of hers. She is not common. She's has come apart from those who are merely physical and ordinary. Another defining characteristic of the Bride is *Maturity*.

In the physical world, there can be no Bride without maturity. Until fully developed, a young woman is not ready for marriage. When her breasts are partially developed, she is not fully ready; she is still growing into maturity (Song of Songs 8:8-10). The same is true for the future Bride. We are developing, but until fully developed, we're not ready.

[Ephesians 4:13-15 E.S.V.] 13 until we all attain to the unity of the faith and of the knowledge of the Son of God, to [a] mature [man], to the measure of the stature of the fullness of [The Anointed King], 14 so that we may no longer be children, tossed to and fro by the waves and carried about by every wind of doctrine, by human cunning, by craftiness in deceitful schemes. 15 Rather, speaking the truth in love, we are to grow up in every way into him who is the head, into [The Anointed King]

King Jesus is waiting for his Bride to develop. She has developed some. She shows maturity, but not completely yet.

If the food selection a person eats is not full enough, if a person is isolated and only gets certain minerals over and over through their food, they cannot develop properly. They will have serious deficiencies.

So the growing Body of The Anointed King must eat the fullness of the Word God provides to it, in order to develop fully. The complete Good News carries all of the "minerals"—the growth factors—for the Bride's full development, so that when she acts on it, walking in the light, she grows into maturity. This is one reason divisions, schisms and doctrinal factions in the Body are so dangerous to it. They can stunt or prevent full maturity. They can cause mineral deficiencies that show and are spiritually unattractive.

We must be careful what we "drink." If you drink continually from a brown, slow moving water source, you will be affected by that. It's *our individual choice* what we listen to.

Part of maturity is how we handle our tongue. Scripture says about the Bride:

[Proverbs 31:26 NKJV] 26 She opens her mouth with wisdom, and on her tongue is the law of kindness.

And it says,

[James 3:2 NKJV, literal added] 2 For we all stumble in many things. If anyone does not stumble in word, he is a [mature] man, able also to bridle [or "control and steer"] the whole body.

There is an elegance to the speech of the Bride, a grace there.

[Colossians 4:6 NKJV] 6 [Let] your speech always [be] with grace, seasoned with salt, that you may know how you ought to answer each one.

She is "groomed" regarding her speech. She prepares and beautifies her heart with good things, so that good comes out via her speech. Her speech can break a bone. It can take down a strong man.

[Matthew 12:34-35 NKJV] 34 ...For out of the abundance of the heart the mouth speaks. 35 "A good man out of the good treasure of his heart brings forth good things...

[Proverbs 25:15 E.S.V.] 15 With patience a ruler may be persuaded, and a soft tongue will break a bone.

Her Bridegroom says about her,

[Song of Songs 4:3, 11 E.S.V.] 3 Your lips are like a scarlet thread,

and your mouth is lovely. ... 11 Your lips drip nectar, my bride; honey and milk are under your tongue...

So the Bride's maturity is in her tongue. She "grows up unto Him who is the Head," by "speaking the Truth in Love" (see Ephesians 4:15, above).

And her maturity is in her perfected Love.

[1 John 2:5 E.S.V.] 5 but whoever keeps his word, in him truly the love of God is perfected…

[1 John 4:7-12 E.S.V.] 7 Beloved, let us love one another, for love is from God, and whoever loves has been born of God and knows God. 8 Anyone who does not love does not know God, because God is love. 9 In this the love of God was made manifest among us, that God sent his only Son into the world, so that we might live through him. 10 In this is love, not that we have loved God but that he loved us and sent his Son to be the propitiation [that is, "satisfying sacrifice"] for our sins. 11 Beloved, if God so loved us, we also ought to love one another. 12 No one has ever seen God; if we love one another, God abides in us and his love is perfected in us.

Less mature believers are at times a challenge to love. They can be like a baby who vomits on one's nice blouse or pees or even poos on you. But the Bride guards her tongue in this situation. She keeps herself free from the spirit of slander or gossip. She "covers," "loving fervently from the heart," because "love covers a multitude of sins" (1 Peter 4:8).

[1 John 4:16-21 NKJV] 16 And we have known and believed the love that God has for us. God is love, and he who abides in love abides in God, and God in him. 17 Love has been perfected among us in this: that we may have boldness in the day of judgment; because as He is, so are we in this world. 18 There is no fear in love; but perfect love casts out fear, because fear involves torment. But he who fears has not been made perfect in love. 19 We love Him because He first loved us. 20 If someone says, "I love God," and hates his brother, he is a liar; for he who does not love his brother whom he has seen, how can he love God

whom he has not seen? 21 And this commandment we have from
Him: that he who loves God [must] love his brother also.

Chapter 9

Characteristics of Marriage & Purity

The Bride is also a "chaste virgin." She is not a prostitute or fornicator. She guards her heart *powerfully*, with the offensive weapon of her speech, to keep predators away. She's absolutely scary to anyone who would want to seduce her, and she does not show herself attractive to them.

The serpent successfully seduced Eve in the garden. But the Bride will overcome the serpent. The serpent represents seemingly innocent, seductive lies. Paul said to the maturing Believers in Corinth:

[2 Corinthians 11:2-3 E.S.V.] 2 For I feel a divine jealousy for you, since I betrothed you to one husband, to present you as a pure virgin to [The Anointed King]. 3 But I am afraid that as the serpent deceived Eve by his cunning, your thoughts will be led astray from a sincere and pure devotion to [The Anointed King].

A "chaste" or "pure" virgin is one who learns discretion. She yields to godly council, from parents and wise people, in order to learn discretion while in the world. She lives in a high tower of security, protected from the serpents down on the earth. Her heart is full of the fire of Love, for her future Bridegroom. So she stays the course.

Discretion also means, "taste," in the original Hebrew.

[Proverbs 11:22 N.A.S.B.] 22 As a ring of gold in a pig's snout so is a beautiful woman who lacks discretion.

All women have beauty; it's the image of God that he gave to them when he made them. That beauty is valuable, so a woman must learn discretion in order to protect it. Discretion is like the thorns on the stem of a rose; they pair with its beauty to protect the delicate and beautiful rose petals from predators. These would include insects and wild animals which would freely come over and devour the rose petals, if they could. A woman without discretion is like a rose without thorns.

That's why it's only fitting for women, because they have beauty, to also have discretion.

Discretion includes choosing who to be around, who to accept into one's life, who to allow to get close, and whose words to listen to. It also allows a person to know what accolades they should *not* accept.

The world will "reward" a woman with praises for her beauty. If a woman develops faster than others in High School, in the world system, those of the world will reward her with praise and then try to *pair her* with a handsome "jock" or "cool" type. But discretion will make a daughter of God stay out of that foolishness. She retains her right to evaluate and make her own chooses based on wisdom. Her discretion allows her to always be in the director's seat of her life, always in charge of her own life and relationships.

Discretion includes the way a woman presents herself in public, her "taste" in how she dresses. Women carry beauty. Its value is great, and it requires responsibility. The Bride of the Lamb learns this. She *has* the beauty of distinctiveness, having been looking long in the Mirror at the glory of the Lord. So people in the world will desire to take hold of her because of that. But she remains above, so she can shine.

When women cover the beauty of their bodies, not out of fear but out of discretion, they are displaying the dignity of the Bride of the Lamb. They also extinguish the fire of some men's over-desire. Those men want to see them in a sexual context, but they can't because of this kind of woman's discretion. So they go away disappointed, and so do the spirits with them. This is the power of a godly woman using discretion.

In the West, the serpent has been pumping a filthy deception into the world, which has contaminated the world's women. The Word of Truth, when applied, cleanses that filth off easily. That enemy, through a deceptive image that he puts in front of the masses continually, has made many women too physically orientated. He made them too concerned about their personal, outward look. His lies and abuse has made them try hard continually to shine that way, to attract attention to themselves. The physical is important, but it's the *lowest* part of a person, who is in totality, spirit, soul and body.

The Bride of the Lamb has more beauty than imaginable, but it shines from within, out *through* the body. This is true for both women and men within the Bride of The Anointed King. We learn not to point people to our outward appearance, but to shine out for people, as Light shining through the eyes of the Bride to the world.

The discretion of the Bride of the Lamb causes her to devote herself to the right people. She is not accessible to just anyone who wants to tread across her garden and trample on her. No, she is as an exquisite, attractive, one-of-a-kind, flower, so she learns to protect herself. Her heavenly Bridegroom commends her for this:

[Song of Songs 4:12, 15 E.S.V.] 12 A garden locked is my sister, my bride, a spring locked, a fountain sealed. ... 15 a garden fountain, a well of living water, and flowing streams from Lebanon.

This kind of discretion and at times, seclusion, makes her compatible to her Bridegroom. When he was on the earth, he did not remain around the crowd. If he had, they would've taken hold of him and kept him for themselves. No. He was physically on earth, but through quality choices of where he would be and who he would be with, he maintained his Eden-like atmosphere and vibrant connection with his Father at all times. This allowed him to always function as the power station, to serve dying and hurting humanity.

If he had looked at the faces and ways of man too long, he would've begun to manifest those ways in himself also—that is the wrong mirror to be looking into. But he related to the Father and the Scripture and the Holy Spirit most, and he lived in a vault, as does his Bride today.

No casual "friendships" based on outward appearance or feelings; those would give access to people who eventually backbite, accuse and viciously throw down the growing Bride-to-be. They will be jealous when they see her shine, and they will try to put her light out. It is *her* job to give *them* the Good News, to shine *for* them and to not need, want or get anything from them. She is to step back after shining for them, to let them make their own individual choice before God. The Bride has a high, high, supernatural path to walk on that's far above, so she goes back to that every time after serving needy humanity.

She comes to know "what is in man," and stays separate, like Jesus.

[John 2:24-25 NKJV] 24 But Jesus did not commit Himself to them, because He knew all [men], 25 and had no need that anyone should testify of man, for He knew what was in man.

[Hebrews 7:26 NKJV] 26 For such a High Priest was fitting for us, [who is] holy, harmless, undefiled, separate from sinners, and has become higher than the heavens

This is the Jesus who was accused of being "a friend of sinners" (See Matthew 11:19). He got close to people and rubbed shoulders with them, but always coming from above, from a high place in the spirit, always as a messenger to them, having Good News, as a Light. They knew he was different; that's why they converted to him and began the long process of learning his heavenly ways.

Jesus' way, then and now, began to break up the hypocrisy of some religious leaders around him. They had a mask of purity, but it was not real. They stayed "separate" physically, but internally they were slaves to the same sins they accused people of. Jesus was set apart internally, but got very close physically, as the cure for people, to relieve and soothe them. He was at the same time, breaking up that religious mask and exposing the hypocrisy.

The Bride follows this:

[2 Corinthians 6:14-18-7:1 N.A.S.B.] 14 Do not be bound together with unbelievers; for what partnership have righteousness and lawlessness, or what fellowship has light with darkness? 15 Or what harmony has [The Anointed King] with Belial, or what has a believer in common with an unbeliever? 16 Or what agreement has the temple of God with idols? For we are the temple of the living God; just as God said, "I WILL DWELL IN THEM AND WALK AMONG THEM; AND I WILL BE THEIR GOD, AND THEY SHALL BE MY PEOPLE. 17 "Therefore, COME OUT FROM THEIR MIDST AND BE SEPARATE," says the Lord. "AND DO NOT TOUCH WHAT IS UNCLEAN; And I will welcome you. 18 "And I will be a father to you, And you shall be sons and daughters to Me," Says the Lord Almighty. 1 Therefore, having these promises, beloved, let us cleanse ourselves from all defilement [or "dirtiness"] of flesh and spirit, perfecting [or "completing"] holiness [or "distinctiveness"] in the fear of God.

One area of distinctiveness that those in the Bride all develop is that of sexuality and marriage. Through popular media, in many countries of the world, the serpent has been shooting his venom to infect the masses. He's been lying. But the Body of the Anointed King ("Christ") is told to be increasingly set apart from those ideas and ways of life.

1 Thessalonians 4:1-8 (literal):

1 "Finally then, brothers we request and urge you in the Lord Jesus that as you received from us as to how to walk and please God (just as you actually do walk), that you excel still more.

2 For you know what instructions we gave you by the Lord Jesus.

3 For this is the will of God, your distinctiveness: that you abstain from fornication;

4 that each of you know how to acquire his own vessel [that is, to acquire a spouse: "the body of a person who truly belongs to you"] in distinctiveness and honor,

5 not in the passion of distorted, over-desire, like the Gentiles who do not know God;

6 and that no one cross a threshold [into another person's house] and cheat his brother in this area, because is the Lord is the avenger [the one who takes revenge and punishes] in all these things, just as we also told you previously and warned you solemnly.

7 For God has not called us to impurity [that is, "defilement—mental and spiritual dirtiness"] but into set apart distinctiveness.

8 Therefore, the one who rejects this is not rejecting man, but the God who gives His Distinctive Spirit to you [to help you become distinctive in every area through the Truth].

9 Now as to brotherly love, you have no need for anyone to write you, for you yourselves are taught by God to love one another;

I'd like first to point out verse 9. The Believers in this region knew to love one another. But they needed someone to point out verses 1-8 about purity. Likewise, where the Gospel is taught today, there is often a lot of good Truth shared, but very, *very* little about abstaining from fornication and acquiring a real spouse. But this is part of the Bride's beautification, her "sanctification," what makes her distinctly different in the world, her perfume.

As the Lamb said about His Bride:

[Song of Songs 2:2 NKJV] 2 Like a lily among thorns, so is my love among the daughters.

So let's look into 1 Thessalonians 4, above.

Verse 1: by learning these things, you will be able to live a lifestyle that pleases God.

Verse 2: because of their high, high importance, these instructions Paul gave were directly given by the Lord Jesus to him, to pass on to them. All Scripture is God-breathed and by the Spirit, but these instructions, even among Scripture, were special.

Verse 3 and verse 8: these things are specifically, "God's will," and he gives his Spirit of Distinctiveness to help us with it. Also, to reject these instructions is to reject Him.

Verse 3: God's will is that we abstain from "fornication." The enemy, who I mentioned earlier, has almost wiped this word out of the English language, in a desperate attempt to keep God's People from awareness of this. Youth don't know what this is. In my generation, I didn't know either. Everyone in the old world knew what this was, including Jew and Gentile. It's related to marriage, which the enemy has also tried to wipe off the map, in a desperate last moment attempt (but he's losing now).

There is a scientific term, "sexual intercourse," that can be used for animals or people. In an attempt to erase the knowledge of the benefits of marriage and the understanding of the poo-like nature of fornication, the enemy replaced "fornication" and married intimacy with the one word, "sex." This is the abbreviation of a sterile, scientific word. By using it, the lines of reality were blurred. There is not just "sex." There is married intimacy and there is fornication—two totally different things.

In the Bible (and in ancient literature), there are many terms for physical intimacy. It is often spoken of indirectly because people of those times respected and honored it; they knew it was sacred and gave it special recognition. (People of most world cultures do so today also). One of the Bible terms for this most unique union is to *know* someone. This is used for married couples: "Adam knew his wife Eve, and she conceived and bore Cain…" (Genesis 4:1). After Abel was killed,

"Adam knew his wife again; and she bare a son, and called his name Seth…" (Genesis 4:25).

When used for fornication or prostitution, the term usually used in the Bible was "lay with." Another term, eventually used for this was "fornication" (where we get the modern "f-word"). It is male-female "intercourse" without the covenant of marriage.

The "old world," actually is not that old. Most of the changes in societies started very recently, after 1948. *Men* could not legally take of their shirts in public or in cinema until pretty recently, in much of the Western world, which underwent a big pendulum swing. The "big screen" was heavily regulated because it carried even more power, as images on it could be detached from reality and viewed in secret. Of course, video prostitution was illegal.

The recent changes brought in a wave of unintended consequences to modern societies, very quickly: abuse, anxiety, depression, suicide, fear, perversions, STDs, abortions, an epidemic of unwanted divorces, addictions, and the worldwide reemergence of slavery—now even worse: sex slavery, including child sex-slavery.

A man who understood the danger of mis-using intimate pleasure was Job. In the oldest book in the Bible, he called it, "a crime to be punished," and "a fire that burns to complete destruction…" (Job 31:11-12).

Let's go back to the beginning to understand the loving Creator's original design for his creation. He gave humanity these seven things, in this order:

1. A relationship with himself
2. A meaningful purpose on earth, a mission to accomplish, with royal authority to do so
3. The "genders" of male and female, each having a relationship with him, distinct strengths, and a part in the mission
4. Marriage: the greatest of human relationships; the vault of sexual intimacy
5. Intimacy: the male and female becoming "one flesh"
6. Mercy after they departed from him—an animal sacrifice to remove their guilt and a covering for their shame (that is, the fear of being seen). In that mercy, he also promised them a Savior, who would crush the serpent's head and save them
7. Clothing, for privacy, beauty and dignity; to protect the mind, after the fall, and keep physical intimacy in its proper context

The term "Fornication" means sexuality without the marriage covenant. All Gentile nations started with marriage, but many devolved into fornication and adultery (for those who have also lost the knowledge of it, "adultery" means the breaking of the marriage covenant, out of distorted, sexual desire and allurement).

Marriage, in its God-given form, is the bringing together of a man and woman, into a selfless, covenant relationship[3] that is for life. It gives exclusive rights, the most unique of which is called, "the marriage bed": marital intimacy, sexuality. In this protected context, provided by God, intimate, physical union is "blessed," "very good," and carries no shame or regret (see Genesis 1:27-28, 31; 2:25). It's *not* the highest blessing. The relationship itself is greater. The intimacy portion is the "cherry on top" of that relationship—God's wonderful gift of marriage.

So there are really two options.

What about what people today call "homo-sexuality"? There is a reason this term is not in the Bible. God does not see it as an identity. It is an act. In Greek, it's called, "ek-porneuo" which means, literally, "out of prostitution" or "out of fornication." This means that fornication (which in the old world was almost exclusively prostitution) comes first.

A treacherous environment of "sex-traps" and deceptive desires, false promises, bait and hooks is first set up. This is a perversion (or "bending," or "distortion") of the loving Creator's original plan. It creates a distorted mirror image of oneself. And the fire of sexuality without boundaries starts to destroy privacy—in our day, this is *especially* through media. From that environment, various other, newer desires are born, including what people call "homo-sexuality."

It must be understood that just as physical fire does not discriminate or ask who it will hurt or what it will destroy, the various distorted desires *attack people at random!* They attack the *innocent*—children when they are very young. They can attack anyone. But the refreshing, life-giving water of the Word can extinguish them for anyone. I know.

The goal of the invisible enemy behind all of these things is *accusation*, in other words, he wants to accuse and condemn the person he tricks. You are relieved of those accusations as you acknowledge

---

[3] For a quick but powerful education on what this is: "The Marriage Covenant" by Derek Prince

them in front of God and agree with him that they really were mistakes. You heal, and by his power, he forces those accusations away from you.

Let me share with you why so many youth in religiously Christian households have been affected by this particular flame. Here are several reasons:

1. The general environment people have allowed in countries such as the US, which is like a marsh with active geysers and mud-holes people can fall into,
2. A lack of separation created by Christian parents for their kids, related to their identity in The Anointed King and God-given destiny,
3. Ignorance of how to deal with spiritual forces when they do show up. In actually, they are way smaller than their victims, but they attack the ignorant. (Demons are cowards),
4. Mockery or judgmentalness of the particular disfunction, which always causes it to multiply, and
5. Trying to be righteous or walk righteously by outward law (for example, "The Ten Commandments") which actually *empowers sin* (see 1 Corinthians 15:56 and Romans 7:5), rather than by what God intended: grace and truth (see Romans 6:14 and John 1:17)

But by the grace of God, understood in all its Truth, we can walk completely free and ignite others with freedom—by the Truth we come to know (see John 8:32). My book For Freedom and my teaching, "Proclaim Freedom to the Captives" help with this powerfully.[4] Don't judge and condemn yourself—you were an innocent victim. Learn the Truth that sets free. In The Anointed King, despite anything you did or went through, YOU ARE STILL INNOCENT!!!

We looked at 2 Corinthians 11:2: "to present [the Bride] as a pure virgin to The Anointed King." This is not to say that all those in the Bride had a physical background of purity. Completely opposite! To the same people, Paul had written earlier about "fornicators, idolaters, adulterers, men who make dirty themselves with men, mockers" and others, and he said,

[1 Corinthians 6:11 E.S.V.] 11 And such were some of you. But

---

[4] www.ForFreedomBook.com

you were washed, you were sanctified ["set apart"], you were justified ["made right"] in the name of the Lord Jesus [The Anointed King] and by the Spirit of our God.

Then in 2 Corinthians 11:2, he said to the same people that they had become a pure virgin. To be in The Anointed King means we went *through the cross* where all sin died and there is no trace left on us or in us. We are all pure virgins (or pure spouses) in the Anointed King, by the grace of God.

Let's look again at 1 Thessalonians 4:

3 For this is the will of God, your distinctiveness: that you abstain from fornication;

4 that each of you perceive how to acquire his own vessel [that is, "the body of a person that truly belongs to you—via marriage"] in distinctiveness and honor,

5 not in the passion of distorted, over-desire [that is, distorted, excessive, demonically charged desire], like the Gentiles who do not know God

So as we abstain from any sexuality outside of marriage, our distinctiveness increases (verse 3). We shine brighter in the world, with more glory. Look at verse 4. He did not just say "abstain"—there is no "vow of celibacy" in the Bible. He said to figure out how to get married. Marriage is the only relationship in which you own the other person; they become a part of you, and you them. God said to get married and have sexual intimacy within marriage—enjoy the benefits regularly, which will reprogram the brain and create a firewall around you to help protect you from the enemy's puppet strings and accusations. This is how to deal with those! (See 1 Corinthians 7:2-5).

He said "in honor." To honor means to recognize the value of something or someone and reward it with special treatment and care. God commands us to honor marriage, to recognize it is special, to value it; and to honor sexual intimacy, to see it as valuable and special and exquisite and to be protected, to view it as as a rare flower found only once in a lifetime, on a high mountain cliff.

Because of the corruption in the world, through the enemy's deception and people's over-desire, doing this makes us stand out as distinctive, and we burn as a purifying light.

Marriage itself has been attacked by the enemy through media. It has been the thing most discriminated against in the media, within the United States. Having grown up in America, I was originally indoctrinated by US TV and movie entertainment. It took years for God's Word to clean the sludge from that, for me. One day, praying in the Spirit for hours, a reality became crystal clear to me: in all of the movies and TV shows I had ever watched, virtually ALL of the heroes and main characters were unmarried singles.

I thought back to old TV shows my mother used to watch—it was the same. I thought of every classic movie I could think of—they were all the same. A few exceptions existed on TV, such as "Married with Children" and "The Simpsons," but those were used to unravel the fabric of married life even further, through mockery.

This was the foundation of the attack on humanity sexually. In the minds of millions of masses, he kidnapped and executed the image of marriage, and the fact that sexual intimacy is good in and reserved for marriage.

The next thing he did was to hint at fornication. He wouldn't come out and show it yet. There were just hints, usually with cuteness or a joke attached. Then he went further, around the time I was a kid, with sex scenes. These caused the brains of kids who saw them to explode with excitement, desire and curiosity. Around that time, magazine prostitution started to grow, so kids saw that too.

Those things resulted in the common abuse of intimacy—ripping it out of its marriage-vault where it had been kept safe—and with that, the abuse of people, including the abuse of the mind and brain.

And video prostitution was tragically legalized.

Those were just the first few, initial seeds of the forest environment of fornication today.

I've lived in countries where video prostitution was never legalized, such as China. The environment is completely different for young people there. It doesn't have the giant, seething, blood thirsty spider in the overt web, faced by young people in America (and the "free world") today.

So what's the solution? Become the Bride. Be separated out from the darkness of the cultures of this world, by the Truth. Single people can overcome the lies planted in their minds from entertainment propaganda, from childhood up. These lies have hidden the image of marriage, and they have confused genders. They have normalized and made tolerable fornication—something that was at one time a serious crime in all nations. Why was it a crime? *To protect people.*

In the treacherous, dangerous environment of the United States and other places today, the Bride stands and is clothed in a pure, white, wedding dress, through supernatural knowledge of the Truth.

Let's look at verse six. It deals with adultery, which is still punishable by death in many countries and cultures today:

6 and that no one cross a threshold [into another person's house] and cheat his brother in this area [that is, by adultery], because is the Lord is the avenger [the one who takes revenge and punishes] in all these things, just as we also told you previously and warned you solemnly.

See the Lord's attitude to dragging sexuality out of its vault of marriage? He *avenges* that. There is serious, terrible judgment for the abuse of sexuality. Though many nations of the earth today have been corrupted to lose the knowledge of this, we can know it and separate ourselves from their destruction.

[Ephesians 5:1-7 NKJV] 1 Therefore be imitators of God as dear children. 2 And walk in love, as [The Anointed King] also has loved us and given Himself for us, an offering and a sacrifice to God for a sweet-smelling aroma. 3 But fornication and all uncleanness or covetousness, let it not even be named [or, "casually mentioned"] among you, as is fitting for saints [that is, "set apart, distinctive ones"]; 4 neither filthiness, nor foolish talking, nor coarse [joking], which are not fitting, but rather giving of thanks. 5 For this you know, that no fornicator, unclean person, nor covetous man, who is an idolater, has any inheritance in the kingdom of [The Anointed King] and God. 6 Let no one deceive you with empty words, for because of these things the wrath [or "fierce anger"] of God comes upon the sons of disobedience. 7 Therefore do not be partakers with them.

We are "the set apart, distinctive nation" (1 Peter 2:9).

[Hebrews 13:4 NKJV] 4 Marriage is to be held in honor among all, and the bed undefiled [that is, kept clean by purity]; but fornicators and adulterers God will judge.

Create and live in an environment that values marriage, that honors it. In other words, recognize its uniqueness and give it a high place of honor in your thinking. Reject the counterfeits. To try to follow a close but counterfeit version is to dishonor the real thing.

Pursue it, recognizing it is normal. The only exception in Scripture is for those especially set apart as "eunuchs for the Kingdom of God" (Matthew 19:12).

The eunuchs for the Kingdom have a special, supernatural gift that allow them to not marry (1 Corinthians 7:7), and it's very beneficial to the Kingdom because of their active ministry. But for the general human race, God calls marriage "very good" (Genesis 1:31). Adam was single at first, but after a while God called his single state, "not good" (see Genesis 2:18). He brought him Eve. This is God's design.

Let the Word remove the enemy's deceptions implanted in your head through his world's media. This will take serious effort. Only the Bride will do this. She will allow the flow of the oil of the Spirit to cleanse her past thinking. Though partially covered with filth of the world, she transparently acknowledges it, and puts herself in an environment where she can receive cleansing, even if there is the potential to be seen receiving cleansing. The evidence of her purification is already becoming visible. She continues to purify herself over a process of time, knowing she will continually see her King Jesus who is pure. His eyes are looking for her.

7 For God has not called us to impurity [that is, "defilement—mental and spiritual dirtiness"] but into set apart distinctiveness.

Chapter 10

She Answers the Calls

Like Esther, the Bride of the Lamb is called up to her opportunity. To be "called" carries the double meaning of being "invited" and "summoned." When Queen Vashti was summoned, in the book of Esther, she refused and lost her place on her throne.

Another example of failure to respond to the call can be seen here:

[Luke 14:16-24 E.S.V.] 16 But he said to him, "A man once gave a great banquet and invited many. 17 And at the time for the banquet he sent his servant to say to those who had been invited, 'Come, for everything is now ready.' 18 But they all alike began to make excuses. The first said to him, 'I have bought a field, and I must go out and see it. Please have me excused.' 19 And another said, 'I have bought five yoke of oxen, and I go to examine them. Please have me excused.' 20 And another said, 'I have married a wife, and therefore I cannot come.' 21 So the servant came and reported these things to his master. Then the master of the house became angry and said to his servant, 'Go out quickly to the streets and lanes of the city, and bring in the poor and crippled and blind and lame.' 22 And the servant said, 'Sir, what you commanded has been done, and still there is room.' 23 And the master said to the servant, 'Go out to the highways and hedges and compel people to come in, that my house may be filled. 24 For I tell you, none of those men who were invited shall taste my banquet.'"

The banquet Jesus spoke about here is "the marriage supper of the Lamb" described elsewhere. These people were minding earthly, temporary things. They will lose those things, and also their place in the banquet and in the Kingdom, next to the King.

[Matthew 22:10-14 ESV] 10 And those servants went out into the roads and gathered all whom they found, both bad and good. So the wedding hall was filled with guests. 11 "But when the king came in to look at the guests, he saw there a man who had no wedding garment. 12 And he said to him, 'Friend, how did you get in here without a wedding garment?' And he was speechless. 13 Then the king said to the attendants, 'Bind him hand and foot and cast [or "throw"] him into the outer darkness. In that place there will be weeping and gnashing of teeth.' 14 For many are called ["invited, summoned"], but few are chosen."

The Bride is not forced to become the Bride. She chooses to answer the call, and continues to do so to the end. Because of that, she will be chosen as the Bride of the Lamb.

The calling of the Bride is continual, because she continually answers it.

[1 Thessalonians 5:23-24 E.S.V.] 23 Now may the God of peace himself [set you apart as] completely [distinctive], and may your whole spirit and soul and body be kept blameless at the coming of our Lord Jesus [The Anointed King]. 24 He who CALLS you is faithful; he will surely do it.

[Galatians 5:8 E.S.V.] 8 ...[God] CALLS you.

It is a calling *to him*. It is first of all relational.

[Acts 2:39 E.S.V.] 39 For the promise is for you and for your children and for all who are far off, everyone whom the Lord our God calls to himself."

[Mark 3:13-14 N.A.S.B.] 13 And He went up on the mountain and summoned those whom He Himself wanted, and they came to Him. 14 And He appointed twelve, so that they would *be with Him* and that He could send them out to ["proclaim"],

The Bride at times will hear the call of her Bridegroom to himself.

[Song of Songs 2:10-13 E.S.V.] 10 My beloved speaks and says to me: "Arise, my love, my beautiful one, and come away, 11 for behold, the winter is past; the rain is over and gone. 12 The flowers appear on the earth, the time of singing has come, and the voice of the turtledove is heard in our land. 13 The fig tree ripens its figs, and the vines are in blossom; they give forth fragrance. Arise, my love, my beautiful one, and come away.

The Bride can hear his call though the Message, the Gospel.

[2 Thessalonians 2:14 E.S.V.] 14 To this he called you through our gospel, so that you may obtain the glory of our Lord Jesus [The Anointed King].

Some hear the Good News as unintelligible words, as a scrambled signal. But the Bride hears a glorious, clear call through them. This call causes her to rise up and go. Her response to him conforms her to the mold of His glory.

Why does he continually call her? Because he is enamored with her beauty. He has gifts for her, a bouquet of roses he can only give her as she answers his calls.

[Song of Songs 5:2-6 E.S.V.] 2 I slept, but my heart was awake. A sound! My beloved is knocking. "Open to me, my sister, my love, my dove, my perfect one, for my head is wet with dew, my locks with the drops of the night." 3 I had put off my garment; how could I put it on? I had bathed my feet; how could I soil them? 4 My beloved put his hand to the latch, and my heart was thrilled within me. 5 I arose to open to my beloved, and my hands dripped with myrrh, my fingers with liquid myrrh, on the handles of the bolt. 6 I opened to my beloved, but my beloved had turned and gone. My soul failed me when he spoke. I sought him, but found him not; I called him, but he gave no answer.

The King of Glory is always on mission. He calls us to serve with him, as his active Body. But if we hesitate, he must move on. He is like the wind (see John 3:8). We may hesitate, but the Bride's longing for her Bridegroom keeps her pursing him until she finds him.

The Bridegroom's call is the greatest of all possible callings:

[1 Thessalonians 2:12 E.S.V.] 12 we exhorted each one of you and encouraged you and charged you to walk in a manner worthy of God, who calls you into his own kingdom and glory.

God calls his People to have and exude HIS glory. In other words, we have on the inside of us the same nature and essence as God, as our inner being. When we shine, it is with His glory; something far greater than anything physical or mental. As the Bride gets in touch with the Word God provides her as adornment, she is preparing herself to display the Anointed King she is clothed with to the world.

And this glory is related to God's Kingdom. The Bride is comprised of those of the Body who will inherit the Kingdom, by not trading their inheritance for earthly things (see Hebrews 12:15-17). No matter the earthly cost, they don't turn down the call. She will reign at the side of her heavenly Bridegroom.

This reign starts now, as she shines actively for the world. But on that Day, at the Wedding Banquet of the Lamb, she will be revealed. She will shine fully with the glory of God, standing as royalty in his Kingdom.

All of the Body hears the call of the King and initially responds. But the Bride continues to respond, till in the end she is chosen by her King, whose eyes are looking for her continually.

Chapter 11

How She Dwells Above the Earth

Answering the callings of the Lord detaches the Bride from the earth, and takes her upward and further and further away from it.

About her it says,

[Psalm 45:10-11 NKJV] 10 Listen, O daughter, consider and incline your ear; forget your own people also, and your father's house; 11 so the King will greatly desire your beauty; because He [is] your Lord, worship Him.

The privileges and benefits the Bride unlocks by this wholehearted act are far greater than any deceptive thing she could try to take hold of on earth. By this act, she is making way for her royal identity and destiny to be revealed, to heaven and earth.

Abraham is a great illustration of this.

[Genesis 12:1-3 NKJV] 1 Now the LORD had said to Abram: "Get out of your country, from your family and from your father's house, to a land that I will show you. 2 I will make you a great nation; I will bless you and make your name great; and you shall be a blessing. 3 I will bless those who bless you, and I will curse him who curses you; and in you all the families of the earth shall be blessed."

To accomplish his destiny, he had to detach from the physical he was so familiar with around him. It's not that he *loved* his present circumstances. In fact, being immobile carries a terrible earthly stench, like that of animals too long in a stall. But it was *familiar*; it was predictable; it was comfortable. Therefore, many get stuck in that mud, and teeter. Their goal there is to maintain their balance, trying not to fall, though they do. They're "playing it safe."

Abraham is "the father of faith" (see Romans 4). He showed by his example how faith produces: through movement, by action, by going. God became his Rock. Like Israel in the desert, he followed the Cloud, wherever it went. Like Jesus said about those born from above, they are like the Wind, completely unpredictable.

[Genesis 12:4 NKJV] 4 So Abram departed as the LORD had spoken to him...

What would God then be able to do with Abram? He could reshape him, mold him, open his eyes to what he would give him, his vast destiny and inheritance. And he could rename him, expanding his capacity to be able to reach his immense destiny. Abraham became like children's putty in the hand of the Master. The Master then had his heart.

Out of the rut of earthly stagnation, the Bride of the Lamb is on her way. Like Abraham, she barely knows where she is going. She leans on her Beloved and begins the journey. On that glorious and treacherous journey, she is given something: Truth. Her eyes are enlightened. This Truth includes *who she is* and *where she's going, her God-given destiny on the earth,* and *her great reward.* She's given the power to see it far off, to proceed in that direction. She's journeying through a desert, but she barely notices that because of the constant supply of Water she continually returns to and because her eyes are on the end of her journey.

The People the New Testament was written to were not today's "church folks." They were on a journey. They were "pilgrims and sojourners" (see 1 Peter 2:11) on earth during this age. Peter wrote to some of them:

[1 Peter 1:13 E.S.V.] 13 Therefore, [putting on the belt of truth for your minds], and being sober-minded, set your hope [Lit., "anticipation"] fully on the grace that will be brought to you at the revelation of Jesus [The Anointed King].

God grants us the Truth of the Gospel, including the short and long-term "anticipation [or "hope"] of the Gospel," to keep us going and ensure we show ourselves gloriously victorious while in the world.

He also shows each one of us our individual destinies, on this greatest of Paths.

[Hebrews 11:13-16 E.S.V.] 13 These [former Believers] all died in faith, not having received the things promised, but having seen them and greeted them from afar, and having acknowledged that they were strangers and exiles on the earth. 14 For people who speak thus make it clear that they are seeking a homeland. 15 If they had been thinking of that land from which they had gone out, they would have had opportunity to return. 16 But as it is, they desire a better country, that is, a heavenly one. Therefore God is not ashamed to be called their God, for he has prepared for them a city.

The Bride is truly nervous about this "detaching" at first, no question. But for the sake of the One who calls, despite anything, she goes. She launches out alone, on her own, at what even seems like an illogical time.

As she goes, the Bridgroom sends her something: "the kisses of his mouth."

[Song of Songs 1:2 E.S.V.] 2 Let him kiss me with the kisses of his mouth! For your love is better than wine

He affirms the decision of the Bride and her growing glory that she has now begun to show.

How does the Bride discover her true identity? The Lord enlightens her eyes to it over time, to her great delight. He sees it, even when hidden deep inside, and his Words bring it out for her.

[Song of Songs 4:7 E.S.V.] 7 You are altogether beautiful, my love; there is no flaw in you.

His Words define her. Although weak to start, she is strengthened by His Words to fit into the image that he sees of her. She transforms into a confident woman, mature and proficient in doing her Father's business, able to display her work.

The Man of God, Mike Bickle produced a glorious dramatization of the Song of Songs called "The Fire of Love" that blessed a multitude of lives including my own. In it, he spoke as the Bride to the

Bridegroom when he said:

"You see my qualities before I've even understood them. You see the budding virtues of my life, and you affirm me, you embrace me. You call forth those things which are not, as though they are. Who sees with your eyes? Who can behold beauty in such brokenness? …For your affirmations, they make my heart strong."

Through the Bridegroom's Words, the Bride begins to become aware of her task on the earth and of her glorious identity. Those words are absorbed into her spirit, so that she can believe and speak them before there is any evidence on the outside. These are the "kisses" of the Bridegroom's mouth. She treasures and stores these up within her. She bottles them. They carry earthquake-like power.

As the Bride journeys toward her goal, which she continually beholds, she actually becomes that goal. Abraham is an example of this.

[Hebrews 11:8-10 E.S.V.] 8 By faith Abraham obeyed when he was called to go out to a place that he was to receive as an inheritance. And he went out, not knowing where he was going. 9 By faith he went to live in the land of promise, as in a foreign land, living in tents with Isaac and Jacob, heirs with him of the same promise. 10 For he was looking forward to the city that has foundations, whose designer and builder is God.

He was searching for that city, which we now know to be "the heavenly Jerusalem." This is the same city that we are now being built into, whose cornerstone is the chosen, Anointed King. We are being built into it continually, as we come to him, and as we seek it over every earthly, temporary treasure.

[1 Peter 2:4-5, 11-12 E.S.V.] 4 As you come to him, a living stone rejected by men but in the sight of God chosen and precious, 5 you yourselves like living stones are being built up as a spiritual house, to be a holy priesthood, to offer spiritual sacrifices acceptable to God through Jesus [The Anointed King]. ... 11 Beloved, I urge you as sojourners and exiles to abstain from the passions of the flesh, which wage war against your soul. 12 Keep your conduct among the Gentiles honorable, so that when they speak against you as evildoers, they may see your good deeds

and glorify God on the day of visitation.

[Hebrews 13:14 E.S.V.] 14 For here we have no lasting city, but we seek the city that is to come.

That city is the end goal, the headquarters of the Kingdom of God. We seek it and walk toward it and give up all for it, and in the end, we will become it fully and permanently.

[Hebrews 3:6 E.S.V.] 6 but [The Anointed King] is faithful over God's house as a son. And we are his house, if indeed we hold fast our confidence and our boasting in our hope.

[Revelation 3:12 E.S.V.] 12 The one who conquers, I will make him a pillar in the temple of my God. Never shall he go out of it, and I will write on him the name of my God, and the name of the city of my God, the new Jerusalem, which comes down from my God out of heaven, and my own new name.

[Revelation 21:2, 9-11, 23 E.S.V.] 2 And I saw the holy city, new Jerusalem, coming down out of heaven from God, prepared as a bride adorned for her husband. ... 9 Then came one of the seven angels who had the seven bowls full of the seven last plagues and spoke to me, saying, "Come, I will show you the Bride, the wife of the Lamb." 10 And he carried me away in the Spirit to a great, high mountain, and showed me the holy city Jerusalem coming down out of heaven from God, 11 having the glory of God, its radiance like a most rare jewel, like a jasper, clear as crystal. ... 23 And the city has no need of sun or moon to shine on it, for the glory of God gives it light, and its lamp is the Lamb.

And our greatest reward will be the Bridegroom, in it.

We become what we behold. The Mirror of the Word works by relationship. It is the future Bridegroom who is setting us apart with the washing of the Water of the Word. The "kisses" of his mouth show us who we are by the Spirit. And this process of transformation takes place in secret, untouchable to the enemy. He can only see us grow huge. He sees the evidence of our transformation, from far below. He has no access to the communication we have with our heavenly Bridegroom or the secret place in which we dwell.

[Psalm 25:14 N.A.S.B.] 14 The secret of the LORD is for those who fear Him, and He will make them know His covenant.

[Psalm 51:6 N.A.S.B.] 6 Behold, You desire truth in the innermost being, and in secret You will make wisdom known to me.

That communication—that Mirror of our transfiguration—works by relationship. When we detach from the comforts of the earth for the sake of the Lord and the Kingdom, we are positioning ourselves close to the King, by heeding his call to "go into all the world…." And he can freely say to us:

[Song of Songs 1:15 E.S.V.] 15 [He] Behold, you are beautiful, my love; behold, you are beautiful; your eyes are doves.

[Song of Songs 4:1 E.S.V.] 1 [He] Behold, you are beautiful, my love, behold, you are beautiful! Your eyes are doves behind your veil. Your hair is like a flock of goats leaping down the slopes of Gilead.

And the Bride eventually can say of herself:

[Song of Songs 2:1 E.S.V.] 1 I am a rose of Sharon, a lily of the valleys.

[Song of Songs 7:10 E.S.V.] 10 I am my beloved's, and his desire is for me.

And observers eventually begin to see our shine and say to us:

[Song of Songs 6:1 E.S.V.] 1 [OTHERS] …O most beautiful among women? Where has your beloved turned, that we may seek him with you?

Chapter 12

She Overcomes Religion

[Song of Songs 2:2 NKJV] 2 Like a lily among thorns, so is my love among the daughters.

The Bride makes it through the treacherous, religious obstacle course, and this is part of what makes her so attractive to the Groom. She overcomes that system and its people by remaining in the "secret place."

[Song of Songs 2:14 NKJV] 14 "O my dove, in the clefts of the rock, in the secret [places] of the cliff, let me see your face, let me hear your voice; for your voice is sweet, and your face lovely."

[Psalms 31:20 NKJV] 20 You shall hide them in the secret place of your presence from the plots of man; You shall keep them secretly in a pavilion from the strife of tongues.

This is how Jesus also overcame it while on earth. The day he was manifested among his brothers they attacked him.

[Luke 4:16-24, 28-30 NKJV] 16 So He came to Nazareth, where He had been brought up. And as His custom was, He went into the synagogue on the Sabbath day, and stood up to read. 17 And He was handed the book of the prophet Isaiah. And when He had opened the book, He found the place where it was written: 18 "The Spirit of the LORD [is] upon Me, Because He has anointed Me To preach the gospel to [the] poor; He has sent Me to heal the brokenhearted, To proclaim liberty to [the] captives And recovery of sight to [the] blind, To set at liberty those who are

oppressed; 19 To proclaim the acceptable year of the LORD." 20 Then He closed the book, and gave [it] back to the attendant and sat down. And the eyes of all who were in the synagogue were fixed on Him. 21 And He began to say to them, "Today this Scripture is fulfilled in your hearing." 22 So all bore witness to Him, and marveled at the gracious words which proceeded out of His mouth. And they said, "Is this not Joseph's son?" 23 He said to them, "You will surely say this proverb to Me, 'Physician, heal yourself! Whatever we have heard done in Capernaum, do also here in Your country.' " 24 Then He said, "Assuredly, I say to you, no prophet is accepted in his own country. ... 28 So all those in the synagogue, when they heard these things, were filled with wrath, 29 and rose up and thrust Him out of the city; and they led Him to the brow of the hill on which their city was built, that they might throw Him down over the cliff. 30 Then passing through the midst of them, He went His way.

He was in a protected, encapsulated state as he walked through them. They could not touch him, no matter how much they tried with their physical strength.

At one point, a blind man was healed by Jesus. Being identified with the powerful Jesus, he then came under scrutiny, and he stood up to the religious system. He's a pattern and picture of the Bride.

[John 9:1, 6-9, 13-34 NKJV] 1 Now as [Jesus] passed by, He saw a man who was blind from birth. ... 6 When He had said these things, He spat on the ground and made clay with the saliva; and He anointed the eyes of the blind man with the clay. 7 And He said to him, "Go, wash in the pool of Siloam" (which is translated, Sent). So he went and washed, and came back seeing. 8 Therefore the neighbors and those who previously had seen that he was blind said, "Is not this he who sat and begged?" 9 Some said, "This is he." Others [said], "He is like him." He said, "I am [he]." ... 13 They brought him who formerly was blind to the Pharisees. 14 Now it was a Sabbath when Jesus made the clay and opened his eyes. 15 Then the Pharisees also asked him again how he had received his sight. He said to them, "He put clay on my eyes, and I washed, and I see." 16 Therefore some of the Pharisees said, "This Man is not from God, because He does not keep the Sabbath." Others said, "How can a man who is a sinner

do such signs?" And there was a division among them. 17 They said to the blind man again, "What do you say about Him because He opened your eyes?" He said, "He is a prophet." 18 But the Jews [that is, "Judeans"] did not believe concerning him, that he had been blind and received his sight, until they called the parents of him who had received his sight. 19 And they asked them, saying, "Is this your son, who you say was born blind? How then does he now see?" 20 His parents answered them and said, "We know that this is our son, and that he was born blind; 21 "but by what means he now sees we do not know, or who opened his eyes we do not know. He is of age; ask him. He will speak for himself." 22 His parents said these [things] because they feared the [Judeans], for the [Judeans] had agreed already that if anyone confessed [that] He [was] [The Anointed King], he would be put out of the synagogue. 23 Therefore his parents said, "He is of age; ask him." 24 So they again called the man who was blind, and said to him, "Give God the glory! We know that this Man is a sinner." 25 He answered and said, "Whether He is a sinner [or not] I do not know. One thing I know: that though I was blind, now I see." 26 Then they said to him again, "What did He do to you? How did He open your eyes?" 27 He answered them, "I told you already, and you did not listen. Why do you want to hear [it] again? Do you also want to become His disciples?" 28 Then they reviled him and said, "You are His disciple, but we are Moses' disciples. 29 "We know that God spoke to Moses; [as for] this [fellow], we do not know where He is from." 30 The man answered and said to them, "Why, this is a marvelous thing, that you do not know where He is from; yet He has opened my eyes! 31 "Now we know that God does not hear sinners; but if anyone is a worshiper of God and does His will, He hears him. 32 "Since the world began it has been unheard of that anyone opened the eyes of one who was born blind. 33 "If this Man were not from God, He could do nothing." 34 They answered and said to him, "You were completely born in sins, and are you teaching us?" And they cast him out.

Being cast out by those strong through religion is a powerful beginning for the Bride, and gets the religious atmosphere out of her system going forward. She then seems to "go it alone," but something always happens. There is an encounter with Jesus, who is also outside of that system. It happened to this man:

[John 9:35 NKJV] 35 Jesus heard that they had cast him out; and when He had found him, He said to him, "Do you believe in the Son of God?"

Rejection from the religious leaders and the people they could influence happened to Jesus as our Cornerstone.

[1 Peter 2:4-6 E.S.V.] 4 As you come to him, a living stone rejected by men but in the sight of God chosen and precious, 5 you yourselves like living stones are being built up as a spiritual house, to be a holy priesthood, to offer spiritual sacrifices acceptable to God through Jesus [The Anointed King]. 6 For it stands in Scripture: "Behold, I am laying in Zion a stone, a cornerstone chosen and precious, and whoever believes in him will not be put to shame."

The cornerstone is the stone that every other stone is measured by in a building. When they rejected the One who God chose and saw correctly as precious, they were cutting themselves out of God's plan and his Building. Those strong through religion eventually do this to the Bride also, who is in the Cornerstone's image.

[Psalm 118:22 E.S.V.] 22 The stone that the builders rejected has become the cornerstone.

Based on Jesus, the Cornerstone, the Bride is being built into the New Jerusalem.

What brings the Bride through all the treachery and rejection, without the smell of smoke on her garments, is that she perseveres in holding on to her love for Jesus. She keeps his image dear in her heart. That's her one thing; she holds onto it even if it means being alone in a wilderness. She stands tall and elegant and holds onto that love.

The bride is actually very weak in herself. But this makes her mega-strong, with ultimate strength. She grows in sincere dependence on her Beloved. Like Jesus said about himself while on earth, "Truly the Son can do nothing of himself, but what he sees the Father do…" (John 5:19). And he said to his followers, "apart from me you can do nothing" (John 15:5).

She learns the secret of utilizing God's strength. As Paul said, "…for when I am weak, then I'm strong" (2 Corinthians 12:10). She learns God's ultimate strength, which comes through infant-like dependency on him:

[1 Peter 2:2 NKJV] as newborn [babies], desire the pure milk of the word, that you may grow thereby

[Psalms 8:2 NKJV] Out of the mouth of [babies] and nursing infants You have ordained strength, because of Your enemies, that You may silence the enemy and the avenger.

The Bride's interest is in her Bridegroom, but in the process of her pursuit, she gets sideswiped by religious leaders (or those in a stupor under their influence).

[Song of Songs 5:6-7 E.S.V.] 6 I opened to my beloved, but my beloved had turned and gone. My soul failed me when he spoke. I sought him, but found him not; I called him, but he gave no answer. 7 The watchmen found me as they went about in the city; they beat me, they bruised me, they took away my veil, those watchmen of the walls.

The Bride is never the mainstream, though she can weave in and out of it to serve them, as Jesus did. She overcomes their speech by her speech of love—she will never stop forgiving and loving them, as Jesus her example did on the cross. In fact, she comes to know that she has been strategically placed *for* them, that they are part of who she is sent to rescue. She does so by shining, even if it's through abuse at their hands.

The religious leaders want to "fix" her, to "heal" her with their sharp tools. But their words, if accepted would actually deform her, by altering the way she sees herself. These leaders' authority is rarely questioned by society. But the Bride has true purity.

The Bride is rejected. But she would rather be like Abel than Cain, like Jesus than Judas, like John the Baptist than the Pharisees, Herod, or Herodias. She would rather be like King David in a cave than King Saul pursuing him from the palace. She knows that in that cave, she has the Light of the Secret Place, and she will never give that up for anything or anyone. In it, she repeatedly finds her true love who she clings too. Religion was never her focus, nor ever will be.

[Song of Songs 3:1-4 E.S.V., emphasis mine] 1 On my bed by night I sought him whom my soul loves; I sought him, but found him not. 2 I will rise now and go about the city, in the streets and in the squares; I will seek him whom my soul loves. I sought him, but found him not. 3 The watchmen found me as they went about in the city. "Have you seen him whom my soul loves?" 4 *Scarcely had I passed them* when I found him whom my soul loves. I held him, and would not let him go until I had brought him into my mother's house, and into the chamber of her who conceived me.

Chapter 13

She Delights in Meditation

[Psalm 1:1-3] 1 Blessed is the man that does not walk in the advice of the common way of thinking, of those who don't worship God. He also does not stand on the path of those who willfully do evil. He also does not sit down and identify with those who are mocking what is right. [He separates from those things]. 2 But his delight is in the law [the revealed Word and will] of the LORD; and in his law he *meditates* day and night. 3 And he will be like a tree planted by the rivers of water, that brings forth its fruit in its season; his leaf will not wither, and whatever he does prospers.

Meditation is *how* the Bride sees herself in the Mirror, long term. It's her regular, Word bubble-bath that she soaks in and cleanses herself in. In other words, it's a continual, lifetime routine for the Bride to be alone with God and his Word.

James spoke of looking into God's Word as a mirror. He first explained why some people don't follow through with God's Word:

[James 1:22-24 E.S.V.] 22 But be doers of the word, and not hearers only, deceiving yourselves. 23 For if anyone is a hearer of the word and not a doer, he is like a man who looks intently at his natural face in a mirror. 24 For he looks at himself and goes away and at once forgets what he was like.

The problem was simply that the person didn't look into the Word *long enough*. He "goes his way" and leaves the image he saw. Because of this, he simply can't carry it out. It's not that he doesn't want to. His nature is to do the will of God. This person's problem is a lack of *meditation*—he didn't look long enough. The radiant Bride, on the other hand, is shown here:

[James 1:25 E.S.V.] 25 But the one who looks into the perfect law, the law of liberty, and perseveres, being no hearer who forgets but a doer who acts, he will be blessed in his doing.

This person takes the Word deposited *inside* of their spirit and acts on it. That Word is alive in them. It is a fire in them that can come out and burn up anything before them. It is refreshing, pleasurable, desirable and bubbles up and overflows out. The Bride sees Herself in the glory of it.

"The perfect law of liberty" is the Spirit energizing and amplifying the Word in us (see, for example Romans 8:2, Philippians 2:13). He brings the Truth home in us, and it becomes a permanent part of our inner being as we do it. It is eaten as food. It is the fuel for our journey that requires we keep filling up as we go. The Bride learns to do this.

Meditation is careful, thoughtful repetition. It is when you slow down long enough to consider a Truth again and again and again, giving the Spirit time to put roots to the seeds (the words) you have received. When you receive a Truth the first time, it is planted in your spirit. But when you go over it again, it is watered by the Spirit, and it begins to grow roots below, for long-lasting fruitfulness above. You begin to see yourself in that Truth. Now it becomes you. It takes on the shape of your actions. You begin to live it out.

The Word is to be cherished. The Bride comes to know that it is the Lord Himself. Its Truth "is seen in him and in you" (1 John 2:8) because it is a Mirror. We just have to spend enough time in front of it, looking into it. This requires prioritization and typically giving up what we would normally want to do. We exchange things for "the good portion" that is actually "necessary":

[Luke 10:38-42 E.S.V.] 38 Now as they went on their way, Jesus entered a village. And a woman named Martha welcomed him into her house. 39 And she had a sister called Mary, who sat at the Lord's feet and listened to his teaching. 40 But Martha was distracted with much serving. And she went up to him and said, "Lord, do you not care that my sister has left me to serve alone? Tell her then to help me." 41 But the Lord answered her, "Martha, Martha, you are anxious and troubled about many

things, 42 but one thing is necessary. Mary has chosen the good portion, which will not be taken away from her."

When we don't just "go our way" (Luke 8:14) but choose to "look intently into the perfect law of freedom," we are literally sitting at the Teacher's feet, like Mary did. And we will grow up into all that he says to us.

[Jer 31:31, 33-34 E.S.V.] 31 "Behold, the days are coming, declares the LORD, when I will make a new covenant with the house of Israel and the house of Judah, ... 33 For this is the covenant that I will make with the house of Israel after those days, declares the LORD: I will put my law within them, and I will write it on their hearts. And I will be their God, and they shall be my people. 34 And no longer shall each one teach his neighbor and each his brother, saying, 'Know the LORD,' for they shall all know me, from the least of them to the greatest, declares the LORD. For I will forgive their iniquity, and I will remember their sin no more."

The reward we receive for utilizing this new covenant provision, is radiance.

[2 Corinthians 3:6-18 E.S.V.] 6 who has made us sufficient to be ministers of a new covenant, not of the letter but of the Spirit. For the letter kills, but the Spirit gives life. 7 Now if the ministry of death, carved in letters on stone, came with such glory that the Israelites could not gaze at Moses' face because of its glory, which was being brought to an end, 8 will not the ministry of the Spirit have even more glory? 9 For if there was glory in the ministry of condemnation, the ministry of righteousness must far exceed it in glory. 10 Indeed, in this case, what once had glory has come to have no glory at all, because of the glory that surpasses it. 11 For if what was being brought to an end came with glory, much more will what is permanent have glory. 12 Since we have such a hope, we are very bold, 13 not like Moses, who would put a veil over his face so that the Israelites might not gaze at the outcome of what was being brought to an end. 14 But their minds were hardened. For to this day, when they read the old covenant, that same veil remains unlifted, because only

through [The Anointed King] is it taken away. 15 Yes, to this day whenever Moses is read a veil lies over their hearts. 16 But when one turns to the Lord, the veil is removed. 17 Now the Lord is the Spirit, and where the Spirit of the Lord is, there is freedom. 18 And we all, with unveiled face, beholding the glory of the Lord, are being transformed into the same image from one degree of glory to another. For this comes from the Lord who is the Spirit.

It's through meditation that our eyes can focus. And as our eye is "single" our whole body is filled with light—the glory of the Lord—that we also shine out.

[Luke 11:34-36 KJV] 34 The light of the body is the eye: therefore when thine eye is single, thy whole body also is full of light; but when [thine eye] is evil, thy body also [is] full of darkness. 35 Take heed therefore that the light which is in thee be not darkness. 36 If thy whole body therefore [be] full of light, having no part dark, the whole shall be full of light, as when the bright shining of a candle doth give thee light.

Chapter 14

She Discovers The Kingdom

[Matthew 13:44 NKJV] 44 "Again, the kingdom of heaven is like treasure hidden in a field, which a man found and hid; and for joy over it he goes and sells all that he has and buys that field.

The Bride is very interested in the Kingdom of God. She gives up "all that she has" for it.

[Isaiah 9:6-7 NKJV] 6 For unto us a Child is born, unto us a Son is given; and the government will be upon His shoulder... 7 Of the increase of [His] government and peace [there will be] no end...

The King came to earth with a Kingdom. He came proclaiming the Kingdom of God. He did not bring a religion to the earth, but God's Country, in the rays of the glory of God. The Bride is interested in what her Bridegroom is interested in, and the thing he came to establish on earth is the Kingdom of God.

Jesus's message was the Kingdom of God. It came through Him, and is available now. This is the Good News of the Kingdom: people can have and enter the Kingdom of God again. Miracles, signs and wonders accompany the proclaiming of this Kingdom.

On her narrow Path over time, the Bride receives insights into this Kingdom. Just as Jesus would have his disciples turn aside and teach them "the mysteries" of the Kingdom of God, so he does for his Bride-to-be.

We begin to understand how the Kingdom works on earth and our place in it, now and in the ages to come. We begin to appreciate our glorious inheritance in the Kingdom of God, and this knowledge allows us to forsake *any* earthly thing for it. Nothing can compare to the immense value of the Kingdom for us. It is "the treasure" hidden in a field.

[Proverbs 31:16 NKJV] 16 [Regarding, "the Excellent Wife":] She considers a field and buys it…

No one on the outside can understand why the Bride chooses the life she does because they can't see the buried treasure that she can see. They only see a barren field, nothing worthy of selling *everything* for. But she sees what is in that field. She is *glad* to sell all for it. This knowledge also sets the Bride apart.

[Mar 4:11 NKJV] 11 And He said to them, "To you it has been given to know the mystery of the kingdom of God; but to those who are outside, all things come in parables

Someday it will be announced, "the kingdoms of this world have become that of the LORD, and of his Anointed King…" (Revelations 11:15), and she is interested in that day. She is looking forward to it. It's part of her anticipation just as it is her Bridegroom's. He looks out over the harvest fields of the earth as potential for the growth of his Kingdom. She also shares that vision and desire. She wants to bring his Kingdom to earth now, at all costs.

[Matthew 6:10 NKJV] 10 Your kingdom come. Your will be done on earth as it is in heaven.

[Matthew 26:42 NKJV] 42 Again, a second time, [Jesus] went away and prayed, saying, "O My Father, if this cup cannot pass away from Me unless I drink it, your will be done."

She co-labors with the Lord by the Spirit, to extend the Kingdom of God into the whole Earth. The Kingdom is his territory, which brings divine and powerful influence wherever it is extended. The Bride's desire and delight is the King and his Kingdom. She loves to see the Lord's will being done, to see captives freed by the increase of God's Kingdom. Just like Jesus said to the Father, she can also say, "I delight to do your will" (Psalm 40:8).

Among other things, Jesus' commission included these:

[Luke 4:18-19 NKJV] 18 "The Spirit of the LORD [is] upon Me, because He has anointed Me to preach the gospel to [the] poor; He has sent Me to heal the brokenhearted, to proclaim liberty to [the] captives and recovery of sight to [the] blind, to set at liberty those who are oppressed; 19 to proclaim the acceptable year of the LORD."

The Bride delights in these things also. She makes his mission her mission. He gave his People that mission (see John 20:21, John 14:12, Acts 1:8), and it is the Bride who takes him up on it. She receives the baton from his hand. She follows in his footsteps on earth.

The Bride is anticipating the Groom's return. She "longs for his appearing" both now and on that Day. She works toward it. There are two major happenings that mark the Lord's return. And these two are related:

[Matthew 24:14 E.S.V.] 14 And this gospel of the kingdom will be proclaimed throughout the whole world as a testimony to all nations, and then the end will come.

[Revelation 19:7 E.S.V.] 7 …the marriage of the Lamb has come, and his Bride has made herself ready

It's through the Bride's active participation in the proclaiming of the Message of the Kingdom in all the earth, to all nations, that she makes herself ready. The Bride "puts her hand to the plow" in active service of the Kingdom of God.

The Book of Acts documents God's Legislature (the literal meaning of "church") spreading in all directions. Those early Believers were all proclaiming the Kingdom of God with signs following everywhere (see, for example, Acts 8:4). The Bride had been launched as a stone from a sling to easily take down Goliath, following her Lord's example. They were "turning the world upside down" (Acts 17:6). And because the Kingdom was being proclaimed everywhere, the end was near (see Acts 19:10, Romans 15:23, Colossians 1:23, Matthew 24:14). Then something happened.

There was a religious, counter attack that came from the inside, through leadership ambition and division. This was prophesied beforehand (Acts 20:29-30, 3John 1:9-10, Matthew 13:24-25).

This religious attack corrupted doctrine and the flowing structure, so that the Bride, who was moving so far, so fast with the Gospel, was slowed down into a fleshly state and stopped. She ended up buried under flesh and giving very little sign of life. The Body became like a powerless statue.

The Bride has been working hard, by the Spirit, to excavate and clean off the lost treasures, buried by the flesh. Those treasures were so covered for so long that they don't even appear to be treasures while being brought back up to the surface.

It's not my intention to proclaim the Kingdom or teach much on it here directly. My goal is to say that on the Bride's journey, there are oasis spots where the Lord will teach her the mysteries of the Kingdom.

In fact, the subject of the Bride itself is a big part of the teaching of the Kingdom. She is the One who answers the call to reign with the Appointed King, Jesus. As a part of the Anointed King, she puts on the apron of service to expand the Kingdom on earth now.

Being Kingdom orientated, the Bride is not religious, but very productive.

[Proverbs 31:13-16, 18-19, 24 NKJV] 13 She seeks wool and flax, And willingly works with her hands. 14 She is like the merchant ships, She brings her food from afar. 15 She also rises while it is yet night, and provides food for her household, and a portion for her maidservants. 16 She considers a field and buys it; from her profits she plants a vineyard. ... 18 She perceives that her merchandise [is] good, and her lamp does not go out by night. 19 She stretches out her hands to the distaff, and her hand holds the spindle. ... 24 She makes linen garments and sells [them], and supplies sashes for the merchants.

The Bride participates actively in "the Great Commission," regardless of whether traditional church around her does or not.

[Mar 16:15-17 E.S.V.] 15 And [Jesus] said to them, "Go into all the world and proclaim the gospel to the whole creation. 16 Whoever believes and is baptized will be saved, but whoever does not believe will be condemned. 17 And these signs will accompany those who believe…

[Mat 28:18-20 E.S.V.] 18 And Jesus came and said to them, "All authority in heaven and on earth has been given to me. 19 Go

therefore and make disciples of all nations, baptizing them in the name of the Father and of the Son and of the Holy Spirit, 20 teaching them to observe all that I have commanded you. And behold, I am with you always, to the end of the age."

[Act 1:8 E.S.V.] 8 But you will receive power when the Holy Spirit has come upon you, and you will be my witnesses in Jerusalem and in all Judea and Samaria, and to the end of the earth."

She will NOT be content with her ministry being like a dusty parked car, with vision obscured by thick dust because of inactivity. This is the sad state of most ministries today. Every Believer has a ministry, and the vast majority are parked in the structure of traditional church, not being used, not turned on, vision darkened and covered with physical thinking, not going anywhere.

The Bride serves. She knows that the royalty of God's Kingdom works through serving (see John 13:1-17, Philippians 2:3-11).

[1 Peter 5:5 N.A.S.B.] 5 …all of you, clothe yourselves with humility [literally, "put on the servant's apron of humility"] toward one another, because GOD IS OPPOSED TO THE PROUD, BUT HE GIVES GRACE TO THE HUMBLE.

[Galatians 5:13 NKJV] 13 …but through love serve one another.

This humility and service ensures that she always promotes unity in the Anointed King's Body. She can never give way to offense because she puts herself at the lowest place. And God continually exalts her.

This humility mends cracks in the Body of the King, bringing about unity, necessary for Kingdom advancement.

[Matthew 12:25 N.A.S.B.] 25 And knowing their thoughts, [Jesus] said to them, "Every kingdom divided against itself is laid waste; and no city or house divided against itself will stand.

The BRIDE is ONE. There is only one Bride of the Lamb, made up of many devoted people. She stays united with the rest of the Body by love, often at her own expense. This is part of her maturity—her preparation for the Marriage.

[Philippians 2:1-5 E.S.V.] 1 So if there is any encouragement in [The Anointed King], any comfort from love, any participation in the Spirit, any affection and sympathy, 2 complete my joy by being of the same mind, having the same love, being in full accord and of one mind. 3 Do nothing from selfish ambition or conceit, but in humility count others more significant than yourselves. 4 Let each of you look not only to his own interests, but also to the interests of others. 5 Have this mind among yourselves, which is yours in [The Anointed King] Jesus,

[Colossians 3:10-14 E.S.V., literal added] 10 and have put on the new [Man], which is being renewed in knowledge after the image of its creator. 11 Here there is not Greek and Jew, circumcised and uncircumcised, barbarian, Scythian, slave, free; but [The Anointed King] is all, and in all. 12 Put on then, as God's chosen ones, holy [distinctive] and beloved, compassionate hearts, kindness, humility, meekness, and patience, 13 bearing with one another and, if one has a complaint against another, forgiving each other; as the Lord has forgiven you, so you also must forgive. 14 And above all these put on love, which binds everything together in perfect harmony.

The Bride participates in "The One-Anothers":

- Romans 15:7: "Accept one another"
- Romans 15:14: "Instruct one another"
- 1 Corinthians 1:10: "Be perfectly joined together in the same mind and judgment"
- Romans 12:10: "Be devoted to one another in brotherly love, in honor giving preference to one another"
- Galatians 6:2: "Bear one another's burdens and so fulfill the law of [The Anointed King]"
- Ephesians 5:19: "...be filled with the Spirit, speaking to one another"
- Ephesians 5:21: "Submit to one another out of fear of [The Anointed King]"
- 1 Thessalonians 5:11: "Comfort and edify one another"
- 1 John 1:7: "Have fellowship with one another"

- **Hebrews 3:13: "Encourage one another daily"**
- **James 5:16: "Confess your sins to one another and pray for**
- **one another that you may be healed"**
- **1 Peter 4:9: "Be hospitable to one another without grumbling"**
- **John 13:34-35: A new commandment I give unto you, that you love one another; as I have loved you, that you also love one another**

The "one-another" most repeated is, "Love one another," occurring 15 times in the New Testament.

The Body is unique and diverse, but united it becomes beautiful, a combination of unique parts, like a quilt. "If the whole body were an eye, where would the sense of hearing be…" (1 Corinthians 12:17).

[1Co 12:24-26 E.S.V.] 24 …God has so composed the body, giving greater honor to the part that lacked it, 25 that there may be no division in the body, but that the members may have the same care for one another. 26 If one member suffers, all suffer together; if one member is honored, all rejoice together.

The Bride becomes least in the King's Body in order to serve everyone else. Therefore, she is actually the greatest (see Matthew 18:1-4, Matthew 23:11-12, Mark 9:33-37, Luke 9:46-48, Luke 22:24-27). She is interested in the Kingdom reaching the world, so she helps develop the Body to make it more productive. It is the Body of the King that exercises his immense authority and power in the earth today. So it must be built up, united, and active in love.

Like the Lamb, the Bride is merciful (that is, "compassionate"). She minimizes sins, calling them sicknesses and extending her hand to heal them (see Matthew 9:9-13, Matthew 8:1-3, Proverbs 31:20). Like Jesus, mercy is one of her main characteristics, and it is the oil that allows the parts of the Body to operate together without friction. Empathy, compassion—caring about and discovering *why* a person acts a certain way, in order to forgive and serve them—these adorn her.

The Bride's finances all belong to the King, and she comes to know that. As her devotion is to the Kingdom, she looks for how she can use her finances to further the reach of the Good News.

[Luke 12:15-21 E.S.V.] 15 And he said to them, "Take care, and

be on your guard against all covetousness, for one's life does not consist in the abundance of his possessions." 16 And he told them a parable, saying, "The land of a rich man produced plentifully, 17 and he thought to himself, 'What shall I do, for I have nowhere to store my crops?' 18 And he said, 'I will do this: I will tear down my barns and build larger ones, and there I will store all my grain and my goods. 19 And I will say to my soul, "Soul, you have ample goods laid up for many years; relax, eat, drink, be merry."' 20 But God said to him, 'Fool! This night your soul is required of you, and the things you have prepared, whose will they be?' 21 So is the one who lays up treasure for himself and is not rich toward God."

The Bride becomes rich toward God, with her finances.

[Luke 8:1-3 E.S.V.] 1 Soon afterward he went on through cities and villages, proclaiming and bringing the good news of the kingdom of God. And the twelve were with him, 2 and also some women who had been healed of evil spirits and infirmities: Mary, called Magdalene, from whom seven demons had gone out, 3 and Joanna, the wife of Chuza, Herod's household manager, and Susanna, and many others, who provided for them out of their means.

She does not have to be coerced into this. She delights in it, and God loves such sacrifices offered by the flame of her fire (see 2 Corinthians 9:7, Philippians 4:18).

Chapter 15

How the Bride Endures

[Hebrews 11:27 E.S.V.] 27 By faith [Moses]...endured as seeing him who is invisible.

Endurance is the funnel that God's People must pass through to reach maturity, to become the Bride, qualified for the Wedding Supper. There is no other way into this exalted position in the Kingdom. For this reason, *anything* that furthers maturity should be seen as a positive thing worthy of *all joy*.

[Luke 6:22-23 NKJV] 22 Blessed are you when men hate you, and when they exclude you, and revile [you], and cast out your name as evil, for the Son of Man's sake. 23 Rejoice in that day and leap for joy! For indeed your reward [is] great in heaven, for in like manner their fathers did to the prophets.

[Acts 5:40-42 NKJV] 40 And they agreed with him, and when they had called for the apostles and beaten [them], they commanded that they should not speak in the name of Jesus, and let them go. 41 So they departed from the presence of the council, rejoicing that they were counted worthy to suffer shame for His name. 42 And daily in the temple, and in every house, they did not cease teaching and preaching Jesus [as] the [The Anointed King].

[Philippians 1:29 NKJV] 29 For to you it has been granted on behalf of [The Anointed King], not only to believe in Him, but also to suffer for His sake,

This suffering is not for foolishness, ignorance or rebellion. It is also not suffering the things that Jesus suffered for us already on the cross. Instead, this is called in the New Testament, "the sufferings of The Anointed King" (see Luke 22:28-30, 1 Peter 4:13, 2 Corinthians 1:5, Colossians 1:24, Romans 8:16-18, 2 Timothy 2:12).

This is for endurance and has glorious purpose. And it is never beyond what we can handle through the Anointed King.

This suffering has two categories in Scripture:

1. persecution, or
2. pressure (typically translated "tribulation" or "affliction")

The New Jerusalem—the Bride of God's People—has streets that are "as pure gold, like transparent glass" (Revelations 21:21). How did they get that way? Through the refining fire of testing.

[1 Peter 4:12-14 E.S.V., literal added] 12 Beloved, do not be surprised at the [burning in you, which is with regard to your temptation], as though something strange were happening to you. 13 But rejoice insofar as you share [The Anointed King]'s sufferings, that you may also rejoice and be glad when his glory is revealed. 14 If you are insulted for the name of [The Anointed King], you are blessed, because the Spirit of glory and of God rests upon you.

He said that there is a burning associated—that is the fire of refining. It's a *good* thing, happening concurrently with the enemy's temptation on the outside. The burning is producing incense to the Father, as you stay submitted (that is, bowing before his Image). And it is refining your faith to make it like transparent gold.

When an expert refines metal, he does so to get the dross up and remove it, till the metal becomes so clean that he can see his image in it. God will see his glory in you, clearly, through the full process of refining.

[1 Peter 1:5-9 N.A.S.B., literal added] 5 who are protected by the power of God through faith for a salvation ready to be revealed in the last time. 6 In this you greatly rejoice, even though now for a little while, if necessary, you have been distressed by various [temptations], 7 so that the [refining] of your faith, [which is] more precious than gold which is perishable, even though

[refined] by fire, may be found to result in praise and glory and honor at the revelation of Jesus [The Anointed King]; 8 and though you have not seen Him, you love Him, and though you do not see Him now, but believe in Him, you greatly rejoice with joy inexpressible and full of glory, 9 obtaining as the outcome of your faith the salvation of your souls.

He's saying that what matters is that your faith make it through its time of refining, which is through various, metered "temptations." How? Keep on rejoicing because something is coming: "the revelation of his glory." This is *not* just when he returns visibly. This is now, to take us from glory to glory. God wants us to see his glory, in the face of The Anointed King. As we do, we will also be revealed as having the same (see Colossians 3:1-4). We are transfigured according to the same image of glory we are enabled to see.

The Bride seeks the image of the Bridegroom—she becomes *obsessed* with it.

Paul revealed about himself

[Philippians 3:8-9 E.S.V.] 8 Indeed, I count everything as loss because of the surpassing worth of knowing [The Anointed King] Jesus my Lord. For his sake I have suffered the loss of all things and count them as rubbish, in order that I may gain [The Anointed King] 9 and be found in him…

It is the image, the knowledge of the glory, the light of the knowledge of that glory, found only in the secret place through the Word—this is what the Bride is after. It is

[2 Corinthians 4:4 E.S.V.] 4 …the light of the gospel of the glory of [The Anointed King], who is the image of God.

It is

[2 Corinthians 4:6 E.S.V.] 6 …the light of the knowledge of the glory of God in the face of Jesus [The Anointed King].

This Image is what we see through the Truth—through the Scripture, through God's People who are serving in Love, through the Word we also speak. We see it by the Spirit. And we can then step into it ourselves, in its various aspects. We are promoted, step by step, as servants of the Word, from one degree of glory to a higher degree.

It is one of the greatest privileges of the New Covenant, that we can now see Jesus.

[Hebrews 2:9 NKJV] 9 But we see Jesus....

Indeed, this is where we are to look when going through challenges:

[Hebrews 12:2-3 NKJV] 2 looking unto Jesus, the author and finisher of [our] faith, who for the joy that was set before Him endured the cross, despising the shame, and has sat down at the right hand of the throne of God. 3 For consider Him who endured such hostility from sinners against Himself, lest you become weary and discouraged in your souls.

Jesus is the image of the glory of God.

[Hebrews 1:2-3 NKJV] 2 has in these last days spoken to us by [His] Son, whom He has appointed heir of all things, through whom also He made the worlds; 3 who being the brightness of [His] glory and the express image of His person...

We endure also by looking ahead to our future anticipation. We are enabled to be "far sighted" also, to see the King in his Kingdom in the future, and us "shining as the sun in the Kingdom of our Father" (see Matthew 13:43). That hope we have "as an anchor of the soul" (Hebrews 6:19). Following it like "the northern star" we will arrive at our destination, *despite any* difficulty of the journey!!! As Paul said,

[1 Corinthians 15:19 E.S.V.] 19 If in [The Anointed King] we have hope [Literal: "anticipation"] in this life only, we are of all people most to be pitied.

No, our hope extends beyond the veil, into our destined place of rest, where we are received by the King of Glory with open arms. We must see our destination, the "anticipation (or, "hope") of the Gospel." By this vision of the future, we can endure all things, *any thing*.

[Romans 12:11-12 N.A.S.B.] 11 [Be] not lagging behind in diligence, fervent in spirit, serving the Lord; 12 rejoicing in hope [Literally, "anticipation"], persevering in tribulation, devoted to prayer

[Romans 8:25 NKJV] 25 But if we hope for what we do not see, we eagerly wait for it with perseverance [or, "endurance"].

We are already victorious, despite what things may look like temporarily (see Romans 8:35-37). Our victory is in The Anointed King. It is already set. It is already ours. We are already risen with Him, enthroned with Him, and hidden in Him. And through our endurance, we will receive the crowns promised to those who love him back (see James 1:12, 2 Timothy 4:8, Revelation 3:11).

The victory works by "our faith," so it is paramount that we not let go of our faith, no matter what happens here (see 1 John 5:4, Luke 22:32, Colossians 1:23). You are completely and gloriously victorious now, no matter what things look like temporarily, physically.

Jesus said,

[John 16:33 NKJV] 33 "These things I have spoken to you, that in Me you may have peace. In the world you will have tribulation; but be of good cheer, I have overcome the world."

And you are IN HIM, securely victorious. That victory is by faith through God's knowledge, held onto by expectation ("hope"), and acted on by love.

[1 Thessalonians 1:2-3 N.A.S.B.] 2 We give thanks to God always for all of you, making mention [of you] in our prayers; 3 constantly bearing in mind your work of faith and labor of love and steadfastness [or "perseverance," "endurance"] of hope in our Lord Jesus [The Anointed King] in the presence of our God and Father

Jesus spoke of two main reasons for His People to endure at the end of the age: an increase in persecution and in lawlessness:

[Matthew 24:9-11 NKJV] 9 "Then they will deliver you up to tribulation and kill you, and you will be hated by all nations for

My name's sake. 10 "And then many will be offended, will betray one another, and will hate one another. 11 "Then many false prophets will rise up and deceive many.

[Mark 13:13 NKJV] 13 "And you will be hated by all for My name's sake. But he who endures to the end shall be saved.

[Matthew 24:12-13 NKJV] 12 "And because lawlessness will abound, the love of many will grow cold. 13 "But he who endures to the end shall be saved.

The darkness will get darker, and this will be the Bride's greatest opportunity to shine, to show her glory, as she becomes brighter and brighter.

[Matthew 24:14 NKJV] 14 "And this gospel of the kingdom will be [proclaimed] in all the world as a witness to all the nations, and then the end will come.

He spoke that the end will be like "the days of Lot" in Sodom and like "the days of Noah" (Luke 17:26-30). In those days people rejected God's plan and warnings and mocked and threatened God's People who walked by faith. Mercy was extended and displayed until the time of judgment, and those who didn't heed the warnings were destroyed.

In that situation, some people of faith were compromised with the world. Lot and his family did not end well. Others were separated from the world by their obedience of faith, namely Abraham, Sarah, Noah and his family. Noah was called a "preacher of righteousness" (2 Peter 2:5). He is a picture of the Bride of the Lamb at the end of this age. Not only will there be increased darkness in the world, *the Light of God's people who are shining will increase.* The Kingdom proclaimers will arise!!!

[Isaiah 60:1-3 NKJV] 1 Arise, shine; For your light has come! and the glory of the LORD is risen upon you. 2 For behold, the darkness shall cover the earth, and deep darkness the people; but the LORD will arise over you, and His glory will be seen upon you. 3 The Gentiles shall come to your light, and kings to the brightness of your rising.

How does She shine? By extending out the Word she so focuses on, in which she sees her glorious image.

[Philippians 2:15-16 NKJV, literal added] 15 ...children of God without fault in the midst of a crooked and perverse generation, among whom you shine as lights [or "stars"] in the world, 16 holding [fast and holding forth] the word of life...

There are two things toward the end of this age that will attempt to *steal* the voice of the Bride, to keep her from shining out her inner brilliance. They are the intimidation of persecution and the manipulation of lawlessness.

In the so-called free world, lawlessness has increased so much that a multitude of women, nearly swept away as by a flood, have had abortions. In the older world—none. The enemy then held a knife up to their throat to silence them from ever speaking up, based on that death.

If that is you, right now simply place your right hand on your chest. As a member of the Body of the Anointed King, he covers you with his long, white robe. You are in his purity and righteousness—pure and righteous. There is no abortion in you. Your voice is released. You're going up automatically and effortlessly now, on pure wings. The only death is the death and burial of Jesus. It dealt with everything. Your mouth is released, your joy of childhood restored.

Now learn to use your voice, to proclaim the Gospel.

[Psa 68:11-12 E.S.V.] 11 The Lord gives the word; the women who announce the news are a great host: 12 "The kings of the armies—they flee, they flee!" The women at home divide the spoil

For any men or women who've been involved in any perversion—it's neutralized. Stand and renounce it. Speak against it and against the spirit behind it. Verbally put up your "no trespassing" signs of purity. It cannot get through the purity given you through the cross of Jesus. So speak that. Also protect yourself by fully anticipating a fulfilling marriage God's way, and by "running away from fornication" as he commands (1 Corinthians 6:18).

The Bride of the Lamb is the One who will endure to the end. She is in a long-distance run, and runs intentionally to win the prize.

Chapter 16

How She Sees Jesus

In the last chapter I wrote that the Bride endures by "seeing him who is unseen." Now I want to tell you one aspect of *how* the Bride sees Jesus.

The Book of 2nd Corinthians chapter 3 speaks about the veil that Moses put on after he gave the Law to Israel. The Law there is called, "the ministry of death," and, though it came by angels, with glory, its glory was fading. Moses didn't want Israel to see that it was fading, so he put a veil over his face to hide that. That veil is still there when people look to that law (or any outward law system) instead of to the Anointed King Jesus.

[2 Corinthians 3:14-16 E.S.V.] 14 But their minds were hardened. For to this day, when they read the old covenant, that same veil remains unlifted, because only through [The Anointed King] is it taken away. 15 Yes, to this day whenever Moses is read a veil lies over their hearts. 16 But when one turns to the Lord, the veil is removed.

When we look directly at the Appointed King, acknowledging that we've already been made righteous and have left earthly law behind, our faces become radiant and enflamed with God's fiery love-essence.

When people try to follow outward law, they miss the benefit of the New Covenant, and they are tightening a noose around their own neck, of bondage actually. Because outward law empowers sin:

[1 Corinthians 15:56-57 E.S.V.] 56 The sting of death is sin, and the power of sin is the law. 57 But [the grace of] God [gives] us the victory through our Lord Jesus [The Anointed King].

[Romans 5:20 NASB] 20 The Law came in so that the transgression would increase…

[Romans 7:5 E.S.V.] 5 For while we were living in the flesh, our sinful passions, aroused by the law, were at work in our members to bear fruit for death.

Paul disclosed about his own life that after he had been born from above, so that he was "alive" and "apart from law," he decided to try to "serve by the old way of the letter" (Romans 7:6). He tried to not sin by a commandment of the law. It was specifically the 10th of the Ten Commandments, written supernaturally on a tablet of stone: "thou shalt not covet." The result for Paul:

[Romans 7:8-11 NKJV] 8 But sin, taking opportunity by the commandment, produced in me all [manner of evil] desire. For apart from the law sin [was] dead. 9 I was alive once without the law, but when the commandment came, sin revived and I died. 10 And the commandment, which [was] to [bring] life, I found to [bring] death. 11 For sin, taking occasion by the commandment, deceived me, and by it killed [me].

Through all this he "discovered a law"—not the Law of Moses he already knew, but another: "the law of sin and death," in the flesh. It is empowered by outward law. And he also discovered the solution! ☺ John, the apostle, named it here:

[John 1:17 NKJV] For the law was given through Moses, but grace and truth came through Jesus [The Anointed King].

Grace (or "generosity") is what God gave us in the Anointed King. It put us "in The Anointed King," so that we experienced *everything* "with Him," including death, burial, resurrection and glorification. Truth is given by the Spirit of Truth real-time, continually. His focused, laser-light of Truth can powerfully remove anything blocking the beauty and shine of our face. As he reveals the Truth, we are in the glory of it, as the cloud came on Moses in his Tent when he met with God. Moses was a mere "shadow" of what we have now, truly face-to-face with the Lord, in glory.

This glorious transition from outward law to inward was prophesied beforehand:

[Jeremiah 31:31-34 E.S.V.] 31 "Behold, the days are coming, declares the LORD, when I will make a new covenant with the house of Israel and the house of Judah, 32 not like the covenant that I made with their fathers on the day when I took them by the hand to bring them out of the land of Egypt...declares the LORD. 33 For this is the covenant that I will make with the house of Israel after those days, declares the LORD: I will put my law within them, and I will write it on their hearts. And I will be their God, and they shall be my people. 34 And no longer shall each one teach his neighbor and each his brother, saying, 'Know the LORD,' for they shall all know me, from the least of them to the greatest, declares the LORD. For I will forgive their iniquity, and I will remember their sin no more."

Those in the New Covenant, including Believers from both Jew and Gentile backgrounds, are under the new system called "grace" (God's "generosity" in the Anointed King). Under grace, their bonds were *already* incinerated—they are truly free. Now they simply need Truth revealed to them, so they can transform in every area, from earthly caterpillar to glorious butterfly.

[Romans 7:4-6 E.S.V.] 4 Likewise, my brothers, you also have died to the law through the body of [The Anointed King], so that you may belong to another, to him who has been raised from the dead, in order that we may bear fruit for God. 5 For while we were living in the flesh, our sinful passions, aroused by the law, were at work in our members to bear fruit for death. 6 But now we are released from the law, having died to that which held us captive, so that we serve in the new way of the Spirit and not in the old way of the written code.

In contrast to outward law, we now have God himself writing his laws, by Truth, on the inside of our hearts and minds. It comes through a personal relationship, in a glorious, face-to-face encounter with the Lord. We may not be conscious of our proximity to the Lord at all times, but we are.

[2 Corinthians 3:16-18 E.S.V.] 16 But when one turns to the Lord, the veil is removed. 17 Now the Lord is the Spirit, and where the Spirit of the Lord is, there is freedom. 18 And we all, with unveiled face, beholding the glory of the Lord, are being transformed into the same image from one degree of glory to another. For this comes from the Lord who is the Spirit.

Instead of the Law of Moses (or trying to serve God by any outward law), we have "grace and truth." Instead of the ministry of condemnation, of the letter, we have the ministry of righteousness and the Spirit. This one is permanent and will never fade in glory:

[2 Corinthians 3:6-11 E.S.V.] 6 [we are]...ministers of a new covenant, not of the letter but of the Spirit. For the letter kills, but the Spirit gives life. 7 Now if the ministry of death, carved in letters on stone, came with such glory that the Israelites could not gaze at Moses' face because of its glory, which was being brought to an end, 8 will not the ministry of the Spirit have even more glory? 9 For if there was glory in the ministry of condemnation, the ministry of righteousness must far exceed it in glory. 10 Indeed, in this case, what once had glory has come to have no glory at all, because of the glory that surpasses it. 11 For if what was being brought to an end came with glory, much more will what is permanent have glory.

The solution to Paul's dilemma in Romans 7, which is the dilemma today of many in the Bride, is in Romans chapter 8. It is "the Law of the Spirit of Life in The Anointed King Jesus." In the Anointed King Jesus—where we are already alive, completely free from sin, free from the old nature, free from the flesh, free from the world—we have a new law, which God writes on our minds and hearts by his Spirit over time, as he leads us into all Truth.

We have righteousness already—by grace, based on mercy. So we can relax with no condemnation and simply expose our hearts to Truth of the Good News. It unravels any lies that cause bondage. So we can stand and walk in the full blossom and shine of the glory of our faces.

Chapter 17

She Shines in the Darkest of Places

[Luke 6:40 E.S.V.] 40 A disciple [that is, a "student"] is not above his teacher, but everyone when he is fully trained will be like his teacher.

[John 14:12 E.S.V.] 12 "Truly, truly, I say to you, whoever believes in me will also do the works that I do; and greater works than these will he do, because I am going to the Father.

The Bride of the Lamb grows to not fear darkness. She knows that everything contributes to her fire.

[Romans 8:28-29 NKJV] And we know that all things work together for good to those who love God, to those who are the called according to His purpose. For whom He foreknew, He also predestined conformed to the image of His Son, that He might be the firstborn among many brethren.

All things contribute to her growth in love, as she keeps her eyes fixed on her Bridegroom, in the Mirror of the Truth.

In Revelation, King Jesus is revealed standing in the midst of seven Legislatures. These may represent a complete picture of the variety of His Legislature throughout the age. He instructs and corrects it here, in hopes that each will consider and understand, and change, in order to overcome. He wants all to attain the "full reward" (2 John 1:8), and not forfeit their place in the Kingdom. As he said previously:

[Luke 13:24-28 ESV] 24 "Strive to enter through the narrow door. For many, I tell you, will seek to enter and will not be able. 25

When once the master of the house has risen and shut the door, and you begin to stand outside and to knock at the door, saying, 'Lord, open to us,' then he will answer you, 'I do not know where you come from.' 26 Then you will begin to say, 'We ate and drank in your presence, and you taught in our streets.' 27 But he will say, 'I tell you, I do not know where you come from. Depart from me, all you workers of evil!' 28 In that place there will be weeping and gnashing of teeth, when you see Abraham and Isaac and Jacob and all the prophets in the kingdom of God but you yourselves cast [or "thrown"] out.

Of these seven city's legislatures, there were individuals in them that Jesus affirmed and did not need to correct. And there are two whole legislatures that Jesus did not correct at all: Smyrna and Philadelphia. Smyrna was characterized by *faithfulness despite persecution.* What about Philadelphia?

[Revelation 3:7-13 E.S.V., literal added] 7 "And to the angel of the [Legislature] in Philadelphia write: 'The words of the [set apart] one, the true one, who has the key of David, who opens and no one will shut, who shuts and no one opens. 8 "'I know your works. Behold, I have set before you an open door, which no one is able to shut. I know that you have but little power, and yet you have kept my word and have not denied my name. 9 Behold, I will make those of the synagogue of Satan who say that they are Jews and are not, but lie—behold, I will make them come and bow down before your feet, and they will learn that I have loved you. 10 Because you have kept my word about patient endurance, I will keep you from the hour of trial that is coming on the whole world, to try those who dwell on the earth. 11 I am coming soon. Hold fast what you have, so that no one may seize your crown. 12 The one who conquers, I will make him a pillar in the temple of my God. Never shall he go out of it, and I will write on him the name of my God, and the name of the city of my God, the new Jerusalem, which comes down from my God out of heaven, and my own new name. 13 He who has an ear, let him hear what the Spirit says to the churches.'

This Legislature is characterized by that open door the Lord put before them to *go* through. "Open doors" were spoken of elsewhere also, for example,

[1 Corinthians 16:9 E.S.V.] 9 for a wide door for effective work has opened to me, and there are many adversaries.

This a door of *service*, an opportunity to take the Good News to people (as also in Colossians 4:3, 2 Corinthians 2:12). This Legislature is characterized by *going*, by outreach, by fulfilling the King's mandate to "Go into all the world," save people, and make students who will continue on to make other students according to the same command (Mark 16:15-20, Matthew 28:18-20, Luke 24:46-49, John 20:20-23, Acts 1:8).

This is the Bride. She will always be engaged in and supporting some sort of outreach and the building of the King's Body. And like her Lord, she can be found in the darkest of places. She grows to share the same light that's in her King's eyes, for those in darkness.

[Matthew 9:9-13 E.S.V.] 9 As Jesus passed on from there, he saw a man called Matthew sitting at the tax booth, and he said to him, "Follow me." And he rose and followed him. 10 And as Jesus reclined at table in the house, behold, many tax collectors and sinners came and were reclining with Jesus and his disciples. 11 And when the Pharisees saw this, they said to his disciples, "Why does your teacher eat with tax collectors and sinners?" 12 But when he heard it, he said, "Those who are well have no need of a physician, but those who are sick. 13 Go and learn what this means: 'I desire mercy, and not sacrifice.' For I came not to call the righteous, but sinners."

[Luke 7:34-43 E.S.V.] 34 The Son of Man has come eating and drinking, and you say, 'Look at him! A glutton and a drunkard, a friend of tax collectors and sinners!' 35 Yet wisdom is justified by all her children." 36 One of the Pharisees asked him to eat with him, and he went into the Pharisee's house and reclined at table. 37 And behold, a woman of the city, who was a sinner, when she learned that he was reclining at table in the Pharisee's house, brought an alabaster flask of ointment, 38 and standing behind him at his feet, weeping, she began to wet his feet with her tears and wiped them with the hair of her head and kissed his feet and anointed them with the ointment. 39 Now when the Pharisee

who had invited him saw this, he said to himself, "If this man were a prophet, he would have known who and what sort of woman this is who is touching him, for she is a sinner." 40 And Jesus answering said to him, "Simon, I have something to say to you." And he answered, "Say it, Teacher." 41 "A certain moneylender had two debtors. One owed five hundred denarii, and the other fifty. 42 When they could not pay, he cancelled the debt of both. Now which of them will love him more?" 43 Simon answered, "The one, I suppose, for whom he cancelled the larger debt." And he said to him, "You have judged rightly."

[Luke 15:1-10 E.S.V.] 1 Now the tax collectors and sinners were all drawing near to hear him. 2 And the Pharisees and the scribes grumbled, saying, "This man receives sinners and eats with them." 3 So he told them this parable: 4 "What man of you, having a hundred sheep, if he has lost one of them, does not leave the ninety-nine in the open country, and go after the one that is lost, until he finds it? 5 And when he has found it, he lays it on his shoulders, rejoicing. 6 And when he comes home, he calls together his friends and his neighbors, saying to them, 'Rejoice with me, for I have found my sheep that was lost.' 7 Just so, I tell you, there will be more joy in heaven over one sinner who repents than over ninety-nine righteous persons who need no repentance. 8 "Or what woman, having ten silver coins, if she loses one coin, does not light a lamp and sweep the house and seek diligently until she finds it? 9 And when she has found it, she calls together her friends and neighbors, saying, 'Rejoice with me, for I have found the coin that I had lost.' 10 Just so, I tell you, there is joy before the angels of God over one sinner who repents."

The Bride learns stability herself, and then goes into the darkness to enlighten. She carries the light out into the night, when others are sleeping, indifferent to those lost in darkness.

[Proverbs 29:7 NKJV] 7 The righteous considers the cause of the poor, [But] the wicked does not understand [such] knowledge.

The wicked "support" the poor *perpetually,* for their own benefit. That permanently disables the poor, making them dependent on such rinky-dink support. But the Bride will elevate the poor to her own status and level (see Proverbs 31:20, Psalm 113:7-8).

The Bride's eyes go to and fro throughout the earth, seeking who she can extend a hand to, just like God's eyes (2 Chronicles 16:9).

She is made MIGHTY to serve, just as her Lord is "MIGHTY to save" (Isaiah 63:1). People are attracted to her by her power, and then they can encounter her fruit—Love, joy, peace, patience… (Galatians 5:22-23).

[Proverbs 31:17 NKJV] 17 She girds herself with [or "puts on the belt of"] strength, and strengthens her arms.

The Bride will take the opportunities given her to learn to serve in the Great Commission more effectively (see Ephesians 4:11-16 and John 13:20). In this way, she puts on the "belt of Truth" and increases in power.

Jesus spoke the following to another one of His Legislatures.

[Revelation 3:14-19 N.I.V., literal added] 14 "To the angel of the [Legislature] in Laodicea write: These are the words of the Amen, the faithful and true witness, the ruler of God's creation. 15 I know your deeds, that you are neither cold nor hot. I wish you were either one or the other! 16 So, because you are lukewarm—neither hot nor cold—I am about to spit you out of my mouth. 17 You say, 'I am rich; I have acquired wealth and do not need a thing.' But you do not realize that you are wretched, pitiful, poor, blind and naked. 18 I counsel you to buy from me gold refined in the fire, so you can become rich; and white clothes to wear, so you can cover your shameful nakedness; and salve to put on your eyes, so you can see. 19 Those whom I love I rebuke and discipline. So be earnest and repent [Literally: "come to your senses."]

He is calling you, sounding an alarm to alert you to take hold of this Mirror of the Word and give him opportunity to come in:

[Revelation 3:20-22 N.I.V., literal added] 20 Here I am! I stand at the door and knock. If anyone hears my voice and opens the door, I will come in and eat with that person, and they with me. 21 To the one who is victorious, I will give the right to sit with me on

my throne, just as I was victorious and sat down with my Father on his throne. 22 Whoever has ears, let them hear what the Spirit says to the [Legislatures]."

The King Himself promises you fellowship with himself, if you will do this. Leave the self-sufficient lifestyle, take hold of "the word of his endurance," and become zealous. However difficult that may seem to your physical body and mind, it is fully worth it.

Chapter 18

She Overcomes the Cliff & Rut

In the beginning Adam and Eve fell to the serpent's lies of temptation. But in the end One will emerge on the earth having maintained purity by her speech.

The Bride today will overcome what I call, "the media cliff," which is one of the things found in the desert. It's like the Grand Canyon of the United States.

[Proverbs 23:27 NKJV] 27 For a harlot is a deep pit [or "chasm"], and a seductress is a narrow well.

This comes from women seeing themselves in the wrong mirror. Foolish men *run* off of this cliff and find themselves swinging from a ledge, barely hanging on with one hand, but they can recover. The deceptive mirror was constructed not by humans but by the serpent.

[Proverbs 7:24-26 NKJV] 24 Now therefore, listen to me, [my] children; pay attention to the words of my mouth: 25 do not let your heart turn aside to her ways, do not stray into her paths; 26 For she has cast down many wounded, and all who were slain by her were strong [men].

God's children need protection from the "ways" of this "strange/foreign woman" (see Proverbs 7:5). Otherwise, His daughters will attempt to be like her, and his sons will forfeit "their best strength" for her (see Proverbs 5:9-10, 31:3).

In the mirror that the enemy sets up, a woman sees herself as devious, as a keen and shrewd survivor, as powerful for being able to take hold of hard-to-catch "fish."

[Proverbs 6:26 N.A.S.B.] 26 For on account of a harlot [one is reduced] to a loaf of bread, and an adulteress hunts for the precious life.

That image in the mirror is a shrewd, devious look—and it originally comes from cold-hearted, murderous witchcraft.

This whole cat and mouse game started from a lack of love and connection with parents. This woman plays with men, like a cat with a ball of yarn, and she has real claws.

I don't justify this woman, but I do understand and love her, as does God. I understand *how* she became the way she did, and I don't at all see her as an enemy. I see the spirit that twists and disorients her and "pulls the wool over her eyes." I also see her free and in her original, great, and natural glory.

In Revelation, Jesus attempted to detach a spirit of "Jezebel" from his People:

[Revelation 2:18-20 N.A.S.B., literal added] 18 "And to the angel of the [Legislature] in Thyatira write: The Son of God, who has eyes like a flame of fire, and His feet are like burnished bronze, says this: 19 'I know your deeds, and your love and faith and service and perseverance, and that your deeds of late are greater than at first. 20 'But I have [this] against you, that you tolerate the woman Jezebel, who calls herself a prophetess, and she teaches and leads My bond-servants astray so that they commit [fornication/prostitution]...

This was a woman that was like "Jezebel" in the Old Testament. But the enemy behind her was a spirit with certain characteristics. The actual woman was just "sick" under the strong influence of that spirit. Look at the compassion King Jesus had on the woman herself:

[Revelation 2:21-23 N.A.S.B.] 21 'I gave her time to repent [Literally: "come to her senses"], and she does not want to repent [or "come to her senses, out"] of her immorality. 22 'Behold, I will throw her on a bed [of sickness,] and those who commit adultery with her into great tribulation, unless they repent [that is, "come to their senses, out"] of her deeds. 23 'And I will kill her children with pestilence, and all the ["Legislatures"] will know that I am He who searches the minds and hearts; and I will give

to each one of you according to your deeds.

By her teaching, she was a "stumbling block." But Jesus has great compassion on her. He gave her time. He disciplined her, but not to death. He wanted her to come to her senses.

This woman's heart, that could contain an image of true love, was captured by a beast, the spirit of fornication.

No girl starts out as a "Jezebel." What happens is that the spirit of fornication sends an abused and deceived boy or man to her to seduce her. That person seems so "cool," so attractive. But he's a deceiver, with no love for the girl whatsoever. The attention he shows her has nothing to do with love or relationship. She is curious as to where this is going, so she gives in to the temptation to let him get too close, into her most private life (the physical intimacy to be reserved only for a husband).

At this point, the young boy—previously bit in his own life by a vampire-seductress in the form of physical or image abuse—leaves her. Being a fool, he was never after a meaningful, potentially lasting, pure relationship. And he thinks that she's like him (just as she thinks he's like her). He has no idea the destruction he unleashed on her by using and then leaving her in her vulnerable state. That was a serious rejection, whether he understands or not, that is used to attack her identity at the root level. The serpent is the one behind all of this!

The rejection, committed in her most vulnerable state—that is what the enemy then capitalizes on.

That spirit is like Dracula. He looks charming and well dressed, but he just wants blood. He approaches, inevitably, and his goal is to make her into a Jezebel—to steal the image of love that would be in her heart. He entices her to see herself differently in the mirror, and to *vow* to never be vulnerable again. What begins to grow in her now is a kind of distorted beauty which is a predator in disguise, a man-eater.

Over time, the woman is hurt more and more in a painful cycle. The initial tragedy or tragedies created a distorted self-image. That shattered self-image causes her to long for something: acceptance, beauty, affirmation, to be wanted. This can also create painful, self-abuse for a woman. It all comes from holding on to a broken, distorted self-image. But that is NOT actually your real image!

[Isaiah 52:14 NKJV] 14 ...His visage [or, "image" or "countenance"] was marred more than any man, And His form

more than the sons of men

This prophecy of Isaiah's was fulfilled as Jesus hung on the cross. His visage—his form and appearance—was distorted more than any human's has ever been or ever will be. He was literally like a ball of unrecognizable flesh there, on the cross. Why?

Because he was taking your distorted image from you, to give you the confidence of beauty and full acceptance, to take your place with him at his right hand on his throne. He gave you his radiance of glory in this process. It is yours.

Consider what this means:

[Romans 6:4 NKJV] 4 Therefore we were buried with Him through baptism into death, that just as [the Anointed King] was raised from the dead by the glory of the Father, even so we also should walk in newness of life.

[Romans 6:6 NKJV] 6 knowing this, that our old man was crucified with [Him], that the body of sin might be done away with, that we should no longer be slaves of sin.

Your old nature was *buried* with him, after dying fully with him. And then YOU were raised from the dead with him—the real you, your spirit. Then you were "glorified" with him (see Romans 8:30). The real you is radiant with beauty, beaming endless beauty, in "newness of life." To "walk in" that means to maintain the knowledge (the image) of it throughout your life on earth.

You carry beauty. You didn't deserve it, it wasn't earned. It was given by grace, paid for by Jesus. It is amazing.

Visual media is a powerful, powerful tool that can be used for good or evil. Remember "Medusa?" She had snakes for hair and any man who looked directly at her would turn into a stone figure. This is like when a woman, tricked by the enemy to think she has a "grand canyon" deficit of beauty, covers over that hole with "detestable beauty" (Ezekiel 16:25). That "beauty" is seduction, attempts to make people bow to her image in worship, attempts to hook the minds of men and take their focus.

Medusa in the media *already* has beauty. She doesn't need seduction. But she's paid off by the enemy in order to increase the deficit in her. It increases because seduction never satisfies. If the deficit is increased in her, the enemy can torment and use her more. So she becomes more vulnerable to the enemy.

The media beast's other goal is to cause a *multitude* of men to fall into that chasm, as powerless, stone figures. And if that kind of man does not resist being turned to stone, he will be subdued by it completely. He will become like an empty shell and live to serve the seduction spirit, at the feet of that image. He may look flashy, happy, popular, and amazing in the spotlight, but there is something hidden in his eyes—the corruption of that chasm, a deficit he can't ever fill.

When God is influencing the media, you'll see women's dignity confirmed. You'll see beauty but not as a dead-end focus. You'll see the simplicity of the immense beauty he created, with contentment. People's value will be shown to be much higher than their physical beauty or their accomplishments. And men will respect women. Boundaries will be in place, people honored. Men won't be portrayed as dumb and seducible. The royalty of both men and women will be intact. Like in Cinderella: her value and royalty are brought out. The prince also has chivalry and self-control, and treats her with dignity. He can handle her feminine glory.

We need media programming that puts men and women in secure places with healthy boundaries of privacy, treating each other with dignity, using patience and self-control, honoring marriage. Imagine: every media program reinforcing these whole, healing, life-enhancing ways. Society will transform to it quickly and become established in it over time.

The curtain comes down on the media beast now—let it turn to stone, instead of the males of our society. That spirit of fornication (abuse) will not be allowed in any household when we never tolerate it in a film or a show or a clip. Its power is its images. But the fire of God in His People's households, will burn through those images, binding that beast-spirit. Children will be able to study in school without distraction. They'll also be able to quickly erase any intrusive images of their past. If kids try to abuse other kids—with intrusive physical touch or images—they should be severely punished at school (expelled). If teachers try to do so, they should lose their license and face jail time. If parents allow their kids to watch fornication scenes (video prostitution), they should be punished.

Video prostitution was allowed into society *recently*. When I was a kid it was extremely scarce. It allowed a ravaging beast into our land that has destroyed and eaten away our society from the inside. But that

CAN be reversed.

I am currently writing this book from China, where video prostitution was never made legal. I'm looking at people walking by right now: children holding hands with parents, everyone dressed nicely, having a simple confidence, boundaries intact, very little public seduction from women; very few subdued, predatorial men; way, way less shattered hearts; way, way less anxiety, depression and suicide; way less sexual addiction, and almost no video-sexual addiction.

The majority of who I'm looking at are unbelievers, but they are better off in these areas than many *Believers* in the West. Why? They didn't give "their best strength" to the spirit of fornication, in person or by media. If Believers in the West are connected to the world, they are also connected to that fornication beast that is viciously attacking and feeding on the world there. It's time for the Bride in the West to stand up, separate, and influence public policy, media and education toward purity, which will benefit *everyone.* We are the Light of the World.

Years ago, when I was learning how to handle the media in the US, my wife saw a powerful vision for us. She saw a theatre full of people (Westerners). They were all staring at the stage, mesmerized. The stage represented the visual, entertainment media as a whole. On the stage stood a beast that filled almost the whole stage. That was the spirit of fornication. They didn't realize that they were actually watching him, not all the trimmings of creative programming he adorns himself with. My wife and I were behind the stage, not watching him. (This tells me that we will replace that evil spirit). Light will fill that place where the enemy stood, and a service will go forth there, for the people.

I myself went through extreme temptation as the enemy tried to pull me back. I was raised in America, as a Believer without a lot of distinctiveness. So I became a captive to that spirit. After choosing the narrow path, I had to learn how to cut its tentacles off and stay separate, while in the world. I learned to use the sword of the Spirit and defend my territory from the spirit of seduction. It is a spirit that is alive but completely vulnerable to Our Sword, the Word we speak. One day, after enduring extreme temptation by that spirit, I saw a vision of myself in my future. I pushed a red button, and I saw that beast explode on a huge scale (like, the size of the US or greater).

Let it begin *today* in your life. Do not tolerate fornication, on your phone, in movies, on TV, or any "out of fornication"—the various perversions that grow out of it. Cleanse your house of them physically, as Israel did of physical idols, in order to regain God's favor. Verbally renounce those things. Don't ever live with a "boyfriend" or get too close with a "girlfriend." Respect boundaries. SET THEM in place. And hold on to the image of true love in your hearts, women. It exists. God will give you to *that* kind of man, to a Son you can admire and be completely free and secure with, and comfortable yielding to. Believe, supernaturally look for, and wait for *that.*

To detach from sneaky abusers of the past, you have to forgive. This has to be verbal and thorough. God forgave you. As you forgive people from your past, in detail, you are creating a clean slate, erasing past abuse. They don't *deserve* forgiveness, and you're not excusing their actions. You won't have to let it happen ever again. Instead, by wisdom and discretion for good boundaries, and by "the full armor of God," you'll be safe and protected going forward.

Forgiveness *releases* ***you.***

[Job 42:10 E.S.V.] 10 And the LORD restored the fortunes of Job, when he had prayed for his friends [who had hurt him]. And the LORD gave Job twice as much as he had before.

[Genesis 50:15-21 E.S.V.] 15 When Joseph's brothers saw that their father was dead, they said, "It may be that Joseph will hate us and pay us back for all the evil that we did to him." 16 So they sent a message to Joseph, saying, "Your father gave this command before he died: 17 'Say to Joseph, "Please forgive the transgression of your brothers and their sin, because they did evil to you."' And now, please forgive the transgression of the servants of the God of your father." Joseph wept when they spoke to him. 18 His brothers also came and fell down before him and said, "Behold, we are your servants." 19 But Joseph said to them, "Do not fear, for am I in the place of God? 20 As for you, you meant evil against me, but God meant it for good, to bring it about that many people should be kept alive, as they are today. 21 So do not fear; I will provide for you and your little ones." Thus he comforted them and spoke kindly to them.

The Bride of the Lamb is "loaded." She is pure, meaning her eyes are focused on the Lamb. She is rich in mercy and in love, like her Father is.

[Ephesians 2:4 E.S.V.] 4 But God, being rich in mercy, because

of the great love with which he loved us…

[Matthew 5:44-45 E.S.V.] 44 But I say to you, Love your enemies and pray for those who persecute you, 45 so that you may be sons of your Father who is in heaven. For he makes his sun rise on the evil and on the good, and sends rain on the just and on the unjust.

[Luke 6:36 E.S.V.] 36 Be merciful, even as your Father is merciful.

[Luke 23:33-35 E.S.V.] 33 …they crucified him, and the criminals, one on his right and one on his left. 34 And Jesus said, "Father, forgive them, for they know not what they do." And they cast lots to divide his garments [He was naked]. 35 And the people stood by, watching…

So forgive verbally, and once the "I Owe You" note is ripped up in the spirit realm by your words, never try to find it again. Your feelings will follow. Let God's hand heal you for the abuse inflicted on you. Forgive and leave them with God to judge. You will be released for your glorious destiny that will affect *many*.

This will heal your soul. And the enemy will find no place in your life. He will have no ability to capture you.

Chapter 19

She Overcomes in the Wilderness

Now I want to share with you how THE BRIDE deals with temptation. Like her Counterpart, Jesus, she *utilizes it.*

There is a Truth that is very healthy to understand:

[Psalm 11:5 NKJV] 5 The LORD tests the righteous...

Whereas the enemy *tempts* people, in an *attempt* to make them stumble, God doesn't tempt anyone (see James 1:13). But he brings us through testing, to refine us for the glorious purposes he has for us on the other side of it. So whereas the enemy is willing to attempt to make us stumble, God is willing to allow it for a time, to see us make it through, tested and approved for more glory.

[James 1:12 NKJV] 12 Blessed is the man who endures temptation; for when he has been approved, he will receive the crown of life which the Lord has promised to those who love Him.

It takes the Mirror of the Word to make it through the desert wilderness. It takes continuing to look at it through the most difficult hour. You face what looks like steps downward into a dark place of obscurity, but it is actually the greatest possible promotion.

Jesus faced this first for us, to provide us an example and to be able to help us to get through it to the other side.

[1 Peter 2:21-22 NKJV] 21 For to this you were called, because [The Anointed King] also suffered for us, leaving us an example, that you should follow His steps: 22 "Who committed no sin…

[Hebrews 4:15 NKJV] 15 For we do not have a High Priest who cannot sympathize with our weaknesses, but was in all points tempted as we are, yet without sin.

[Hebrews 2:18 NKJV] 18 For in that He Himself has suffered, being tempted, He is able to aid those who are tempted.

Jesus went through major temptation and testing in the desert. First, let's understand that His time there was *compulsory*.

[Mark 1:9-13 NKJV] 9 It came to pass in those days [that] Jesus came from Nazareth of Galilee, and was baptized by John in the Jordan. 10 And immediately, coming up from the water, He saw the heavens parting and the Spirit descending upon Him like a dove. 11 Then a voice came from heaven, "You are My beloved Son, in whom I am well pleased." 12 Immediately the Spirit drove Him into the wilderness. 13 And He was there in the wilderness forty days, tempted by Satan, and was with the wild beasts; and the angels ministered to Him.

It is compulsory at time for us also. It is called in Scripture, "the time of temptation" (Luke 8:13) and "the evil day" (Ephesians 6:13). Everything Jesus went through, except for the payment for sin and death, serves as an example for us (see Hebrews 12:2-3).

This is GOOD NEWS. Jesus stayed victorious in the wilderness, so by following in His footsteps, we will too. So how did he do it? Here are seven footsteps of Jesus' dealing with temptation:

First, he *prepared* for it beforehand through the Word and relationship with his Father. By this, he was building up faith as a shield, for defense. We are always "protected by the power of God through faith" (1 Peter 1:5), so this is vital. Faith is in the heart, and it has *nothing* to do with feelings. So when feelings change around you, by faith you will stay steady. Exposure to the Word is what gives us faith in our hearts (Romans 10:17).

Jesus was full of fresh, living Water of the Word when he went into the desert. So he didn't run out.

Second, he went in with the right, positive attitude of *expectation*! Part of what the Word did in his heart was give him expectation in his mind. Otherwise called, "the helmet of hope," this is a positive picture of the future he would attain.

He went into the desert *with an aggressive attitude* and *full confidence,* with "the full armor of God"!!! He knew, supernaturally, that this period of temptation was for good. He knew he could utilize it, that he would come out differently, that this was an irreplaceable opportunity. He didn't try to bypass this time. He went into it on the offense.

Third, he *fasted*, to maintain his focus.

[Matthew 4:1-2 NKJV] 1 Then Jesus was led up by the Spirit into the wilderness to be tempted by the devil. 2 And when He had fasted forty days and forty nights, afterward He was hungry.

This is paramount. In the ONE example of Jesus facing prolonged temptation, *he fasted.* As our Example, he was showing us that *this is one of the key elements to winning.*

The Bride mimics her Bridegroom. She is pure and follows him perfectly, as in a mirror. What he does, she does. So she gets the same results.

Fasting is a big subject in the whole Bible. And it is easily either neglected or misused. It is both underemphasized and overemphasized. However, there are several, legitimate reasons to fast. The greatest, in my opinion, is this one: to stabilize oneself and one's focus during the time of temptation.

This kind of fasting slows the enemy's movements way down, reveals his whereabouts and takes away his element of surprise.

The enemy works by schemes and lies, which we deal with by alertness and Truth. Fasting keeps us alert and intentional in finding and continuing in the Truth. It is the Word that makes us giants to the enemy, as we see ourselves the way we really are, in it. Jesus prepared himself to go into the wilderness by the Word.

You can fast one meal. You can fast all beverages except water. You can fast coffee or tea. You can fast meat. You can fast all food. You can fast all food and drink. But *take up this key to win* in the time of heavy temptation, as Jesus did.

Fourth, he *recognized* the enemy. The devil is invisible, and he tries to remain hidden, like a serpent under a board. He is subtle. But Jesus recognized the enemy's suggestions, words, and feelings. He didn't miss or ignore them but responded with full force to overcome him.

Fifth, Jesus *responded* by *continuing to look at the Word*, despite the enemy's smokescreens of deception. The enemy always comes to get you to doubt or question the Word, especially about your identity and victory. It is "your faith" that's being tested and refined. So you must refer back to the Word whenever it's questioned, and its glory rays will stream down and deal with whatever darkness is challenging it.

Never entertain a conversation with the enemy; never mentally go down a path started with a question of unbelief, accusation, or compromise. Always refer back to the Word. You will need the Truth in the right area, to deal with whatever scheme the enemy is trying use on you. Whatever area that is, tighten it up with the Word for that area. This is how you utilize the enemy's temptation. He attempts to strike at any perceived weakness of ours. But by this response, we end up stronger in that exact area than ever before.

Sixth, he also *responded verbally*, with the spoken Word. This was the extension of the "double edged sword" out of Jesus' mouth (Revelation 1:16, 2:12). The Word is as sharp as laser (see Hebrews 4:12), and when spoken can cut down strongholds in the mind easily.

This is the only offensive, hand-to-hand, combat weapon listed in "the full armor of God":

[Ephesians 6:17 NKJV, literal added] 17 And take the helmet of salvation, and the sword of the Spirit, which is the [verbally spoken word[5]] of God

When the enemy comes in a foolish attempt to get you off track, see and *speak* the Word of God. It will go directly into him as he has *no armor* (see Colossians 2:15). Jesus persisted in this until the devil left. That enemy *could not take* any more of the Truth. It will be the same for you if you take up the full armor including the sword: the Word spoken out of YOUR mouth.

[James 4:7 NKJV] 7 Therefore submit to God. Resist the devil and he will flee from you.

I'll give you an example. A daughter of mine in the faith was suddenly surrounded by an "attack" (a mere *attempt*) of the enemy against her. Her feelings started to go haywire. But she was full of the Word. How did she respond? By recording an audio edition of one of my books, that she had been planning to do. As she did, her

---

[5] Greek, "*Rhema*," which means a "*spoken word*" (Strongs Concordance)

atmosphere cleared fully. Those spoken Words she was emitting were like sharp razors against the enemy's poison he had sprayed into her atmosphere. And a razor-sharp net went on and into the enemy's exposed face (he has no armor). So, he ran.

It was not the Word she meditated on that cut through the enemy. Meditation provides the image, but only *speaking* it deals with the tempter who challenges the Truth. It is your offensive power, how you wield the sword.

What is the **Seventh** footstep we get to follow in?

[Luke 4:12-15 NKJV, emphasis mine] 12 And Jesus answered and said to him… 13 Now when the devil had ended every temptation, he departed from Him until an opportune time. 14 Then Jesus *RETURNED IN THE POWER OF THE SPIRIT* to Galilee, and news of Him went out through all the surrounding region. 15 And He taught in their synagogues, being glorified by all.

He had been tested thoroughly. The enemy's temptations didn't work on him. Then he blasted through the enemy. He had become a powerful tool in the Father's hand, for the harvest. The same happens for the Bride.

Chapter 20

Something Happens to Her in the Desert

Was it worth it for King Jesus to have to undergo so much temptation and testing in the desert? His endurance benefitted Israel and the whole world, down to us today and future generations to come. What about for Jesus personally? What it worth it? Yes!!!

[Hebrews 2:17-18 N.A.S.B.] 17 Therefore, He had to be made like His brethren in all things, so that He might become a merciful and faithful high priest in things pertaining to God, to make propitiation for the sins of the people. 18 For since He Himself was tempted in that which He has suffered, He is able to come to the aid of those who are tempted.

By his endurance in the desert, he developed more compassion ("mercy") to be able to serve better.

Like her Counterpart, the Bride also endures the wilderness fully, and comes out exuding the light of the glory of the Bridegroom.

The Bride's transformation from glory to glory is continuous (see 2 Corinthians 3:18). *The wilderness cannot stop it.* Instead, it serves to intensify it because she adjusts and increases her focus.

[2 Corinthians 4:16-18 N.A.S.B.] 16 Therefore we do not lose heart, but though our outer man is decaying, yet our inner man is being renewed day by day. 17 For momentary, light affliction is producing for us an eternal weight of glory far beyond all comparison, 18 while we look not at the things which are seen, but at the things which are not seen; for the things which are seen are temporal, but the things which are not seen are eternal.

Using a magnifying glass to increase the focus of light can make it strong enough to start a fire on a field. The Bride will start fires with the increased focus of light from her eyes.

What does she see there, that others' eyes cannot see? The Lord in His Glory. He is there with her the whole time. Though she is pure, she would give up without him, in that dark time of night. He upholds her and serves her with water for her feet when need be.

In the midst of suffering, the Bride's face shines. She is seeing the face of her Bridegroom, blazing like the brightness of the sun. So her face also blazes like the sun.

Temptation itself, like what Jesus put down in the wilderness, is a form of tribulation (or "pressure"). Tribulation and persecution are two forms of suffering that God's People must sometimes pass through, in the "desert." But the desert does not have to considered a negative thing—it is not. It can be considered pure joy. How? By our focus.

Whatever we focus on is magnified in our eyes. And by focusing on one thing, every other thing goes out of focus and diminishes. Any difficulty becomes "light and momentary." They really are, in the light of clear comparison (see Romans 8:18). The Bride keeps focusing on her Groom.

In Chapter 14 I said that the Bride is One. She is the unified Body, but she is first and foremost One with her Head, Jesus (see 1 Corinthians 6:17). This is why she bears fruit at all times (see Romans 7:4). The desert cannot prevent that. It only serves to make the fruit more exquisite.

There is a Mirror set up for the Bride in the desert. It has the image of the Lord, which she transforms to, causing her glory to increase. She sees what he is really like—things about him the crowd will never understand (see Song of Songs 5:9-16). And this prepares her to serve in the same way.

Nothing can stop the Bride's full shine. The wilderness just serves to contribute to it. She endures fully to be fully conformed to the image of the One she can see shining regardless of circumstance, till one Day she appears before him in the fullness of her divine glory.

So what happens to the Bride in the desert? She grows into maturity, to become an upright and "fruitful vine." She absorbs and utilizes the blazing sun's light, enhancing herself by it, beautifying herself in it.

[James 1:2-4 NKJV, literal added] 2 My brethren, count it all joy

when you fall into various [temptations], 3 knowing that the testing of your faith produces [endurance]. 4 But let [endurance] have [its complete] work, that you may be [mature] and [whole], lacking nothing.

The Bride becomes adorned in the desert. She learns to scatter the wild animals with the fire she's been given to carry. She stands victorious over the physical. She no longer resembles the Adamic race but the risen New Man, the Anointed King. She is the Lion now while still in the desert and consciously one with Him.

The bride becomes vulnerable in the time of temptation. And she is shown to be pure. She shines most beautifully in that darkness of night. Here it is that she learns to "dwell on her high places" (Psalm 18:33). She proves that she can walk on the edge confidently and easily. She was stripped of support other than the Word. She was thereby forced to trust fully in her Lord, to not be caused to fall. And she does.

She went through a dark period similar to Jonah in the whale. And she comes out of that difficult time of inward temptation with great ability to endure. She comes out equipped for the work God is promoting her to.

Chapter 21

You Don't Know the Bride

The Bride of the Lamb does not typically come from royalty.

[1 Corinthians 1:26-30 E.S.V.] 26 For consider your calling, brothers: not many of you were wise according to worldly standards, not many were powerful, not many were of noble birth. 27 But God chose what is foolish in the world to shame the wise; God chose what is weak in the world to shame the strong; 28 God chose what is low and despised in the world, even things that are not, to bring to nothing things that are, 29 so that no human being might boast in the presence of God. 30 And because of him you are in [The Anointed King] Jesus, who became to us wisdom from God, righteousness and [distinctiveness] and redemption

[1 Corinthians 6:9-11 E.S.V.] 9 ...neither [fornicators], nor idolaters, nor adulterers, nor men who [make themselves dirty with men], 10 nor thieves, nor the greedy, nor drunkards, nor [mockers, that is, the verbally abusive], nor [thugs] will inherit the kingdom of God. 11 And such were some of you. But you were washed, you were [set apart], you were [made right] in the name of the Lord Jesus [The Anointed King] and by the Spirit of our God.

The Bride is *elevated* into her royal position, by the generosity of God. Like Esther, she is brought into her position from the outside, by calling of God.

[1 Samuel 2:8 E.S.V.] 8 [The LORD] raises up the poor from the dust; he lifts the needy from the ash heap to make them sit with

princes and inherit a seat of honor. For the pillars of the earth are the LORD's, and on them he has set the world.

[1 Peter 2:9-10 E.S.V.] 9 ...[He] called you out of darkness into his marvelous light. 10 Once you were not a people, but now you are God's people; once you had not received mercy, but now you have received mercy.

The Bride doesn't always *look* good (see Song of Songs 1:5-6). But the KING sees the treasure in her, always, during all of her development and her stumbles in the wilderness. He sees her glory that she cannot see, and communicates it to her like this:

[Song of Songs 1:8 E.S.V.] 8 ...O MOST BEAUTIFUL AMONG WOMEN...

[Song of Songs 1:15 E.S.V.] 15 Behold, you are beautiful, my love; behold, you are beautiful; your eyes are doves.

[Song of Songs 2:10 E.S.V.] 10 ..."Arise, my love, my beautiful one, and come away

[Song of Songs 4:1 E.S.V.] 1 [He] Behold, you are beautiful, my love, behold, you are beautiful! Your eyes are doves behind your veil. Your hair is like a flock of goats leaping down the slopes of Gilead.

[Song of Songs 4:7 N.A.S.B.] 7 "You are altogether beautiful, my darling, and there is no blemish in you.

[Song of Songs 6:4 E.S.V.] 4 [He] You are beautiful as Tirzah, my love, lovely as Jerusalem, awesome as an army with banners.

[Song of Songs 7:6 E.S.V.] 6 How beautiful and pleasant you are, O loved one, with all your delights!

The Bride faces *every* possible obstacle on her way to fulfilling her destiny. What would completely take out an earthly person, cannot take her out. She rises with a strength and resolve the enemy has never seen, except in her Master, Jesus while he was on earth. There is no one like the Bride. She cannot be fully comprehended; but I am allowed to give a snapshot of her glory here.

She goes out beyond. For the love of her bridegroom, she goes way beyond the crowd of her initial companions. He loves that about her. He sees His image in her—that of the Lion of Judah. Just as there is no one like Him, there is also no one like Her.

She endures, till eventually those who would be blinded with a full look at her glory, cry out:

[Song of Songs 8:5 NKJV] 5 Who is this coming up from the wilderness…

The Bridegroom recognizes her. He was waiting for her. But even he has not seen her fully. No groom is allowed by the father of the bride, to see her before the wedding day. So it is with our Bridegroom (see, for example, Song of Songs 4:1). He is waiting, and even he "does not know the day or hour" that she will be ready and revealed.

[Revelation 19:6-8 E.S.V.] 6 Then I heard what seemed to be the voice of a great multitude, like the roar of many waters and like the sound of mighty peals of thunder, crying out, "Hallelujah! For the Lord our God the Almighty reigns. 7 Let us rejoice and exult and give him the glory, for the marriage of the Lamb has come, and his Bride has made herself ready; 8 it was granted her to clothe herself with fine linen, bright and pure"—for the fine linen is the righteous deeds of the saints.

The white wedding dress is radiant and full of her bright glory. It is like the transfigured clothing of the Lord on the mountain when he was revealed in his Kingdom to three disciples—his appearance was like lightning, whiter than any bleach could ever whiten. On that Day, the Bride will stand one last time in front of that Mirror and make a final adjustment. Her preparation is complete. She is now ready.

She must see herself fully first, in His Image, in preparation, before he can fully look upon her.

God is the God of the climax. He is not the God of the "anti-climax." He "saves the best for last," always (John 2:10). Eve is a picture of the Bride. She was created inside of Adam, when God "breathed into him the breath of *lives*" (literal of Genesis 2:7). But she was created hidden. The world and the spiritual realm were not privileged to see her until she was taken out of Adam and brought to him. She was granted the glory of God in such a bright, splendorous and glorious way as she fully carries the beauty element of God.

She was the most powerful. She was made as a companion and *helper* to the man, which reveals that she was more powerful than Adam, as he needed her help. The man, as leader, was to create an environment for her and provide an example.

Similarly, the Bride of the Lamb is more powerful than Jesus was in Israel.

[John 14:12 E.S.V.] 12 "Truly, truly, I say to you, whoever believes in me will also do the works that I do [in context: miracles]; and greater works than these will he do, because I am going to the Father.

When fully trained, she is "like her teacher." She has the same fire of light in her eyes as him.

[Luke 6:40 E.S.V.] 40 A disciple is not above his teacher, but everyone when he is fully trained will be like his teacher.

She is not above him, but she will do greater works, shining brighter and farther, being sent into all the world for every nation.

Meekness is strength under control. Why is the woman under authority, when married? Not for suppression or domination—a perverted mistreatment of forced submission. That is an abuse of authority and the opposite of God's intent. He put her under authority for protection and for more grace. The husband was to provide the ability, through protection and leadership, for her to achieve her greatness. Her highest greatness could come through yielding to Adam, in view of God, because He "exalts the humble." Adam's leadership was to be a launching pad for her.

An "excellent and outstanding wife," described in Proverbs 31, lifts up her husband. He needs her to do so. God sent him someone who is stronger in certain areas, to help him in that way. This kind of woman senses her ability and responsibility to support him, and as a result, "Her husband is known in the gates, when he sits among the elders [that is, the leaders] of the land" (Proverbs 31:23).

She is not just out on her own lifting herself up, but by *serving*, her brightness can be seen in heaven and earth. God's way of promotion in

His kingdom is by serving. She is part of God's help to prepare her husband for his royal service. And together, they both bring glory to their Head, Jesus, and to the Father. The wife's efforts to lift her husband result in God's excellent, surpassing glory and lifting for her, in her royal service.

The same is true for the Bride as a whole. She is the One who is lifting up and seeking the glory of her Head at all times.

The Bride "can do nothing apart from" the Lord Jesus (John 15:5). She is learning, daily, to yield to him. To depart from the Head's instructions in order to do one's own thing would be to disconnect from the power and life of God.

The Bride making herself ready is the marker of the Lord's return. He is waiting for her. Her final preparations for his return signal the immediate coming of the Day of the Lord. This age will be closing as she is completing her work of bringing the Message of the Kingdom to the very last part of the earth.

In Psalm 27, King David said "one thing I have asked of the LORD," and it was to dwell with Him and to "gaze upon the beauty of the LORD." As amazing as our glorious Lord and Savior and King Jesus is, to see the fullness of God's beauty you must see the King's Bride. Like Eve, his Bride is taken out of Him and will display the Beauty side of the Father.

King Jesus alone does not fully express the image and glory of God.[6] Just as with Adam and Eve, he and his Bride do so *together*. They make up the fulness of The Anointed King—He as the risen Head and She as the Body risen with and faithful to Him.

[Genesis 1:27 N.A.S.B.] 27 So God created man in His own image, in the image of God He created him; male and female He created them.

If you are the Bride, you are currently "in" the New Man, hidden inside of the Anointed King. He is "in a deep sleep" away from the earth at this time. And you are developing to be brought out in the end. If you are the Bride, you are a secret weapon. At times you can be seen, as the kicks of baby in a pregnant mother's womb.

---

[6] See, for example, Colossians 1:15,18; Hebrews 1:3,6; John 17:22; Romans 8:16-17, 28-30; 2 Thessalonians 2:14

The Bride of the Lamb is the SECRET WEAPON, and she will be revealed fully to the world before the Lord's return, as she is being "brought to the [New] Man" (Genesis 2:22) by her Father.

She is of him—Man—but different. She is just like him, having been made from his risen Body.[7] She is a Lioness, as he is the Lion. And she wears a crown on her head like his, one of both thorns and of glory.

You do not know the Bride of the Lamb; she is veiled (Song of Songs 4:1, 3, 5:7, 6:7).

Jesus, the Head, "nourishes and cherishes" his whole Body. The Bride is made up of those who fully receive the washing of water with the Word. They look long and full into the light they can see in that Mirror, till there is no spot or blemish or wrinkle—they conform to the image of the Son they can see.

Jesus said, "If you continue in my Word, then you are truly students (or "disciples") of mine, and you will know the Truth, and the Truth will free you" (John 8:31). The Bride is the one who does this, till the power of the Word purifies her and her service is revealed to mankind. The light of the glorious Good News shines for her and gives her ability to walk as his Student.

Mary Magdalene is one picture of the Bride. She was extreme. She started out being freed by Jesus from "seven demons" (Luke 8:2). She obviously "loved much" (Luke 7:47). She traveled with Jesus as he went city to city and village to village proclaiming the Good News, and she supported the work financially (Luke 8:1-3, Mark 15:41). She was one of the few to stay with Jesus through his crucifixion (Mark 15:40). She was one of two sitting opposite Jesus' tomb when the stone was rolled in front of it (Matthew 27:61). On the first day of the week, she was one of three women that went to anoint his body with spices (thinking he was still dead). When they saw that the stone had been rolled away by an angel, they went and brought Peter and John.

Eventually, "the disciples went away to their own homes," but she stayed at the tomb. Apparently, left alone there,

[John 20:11-17 NKJV] 11 But Mary stood outside by the tomb weeping, and as she wept she stooped down [and looked] into

[7] The only difference is that He redeemed Her to become a part of Himself, His Body, of which He is the Head

the tomb. 12 And she saw two angels in white sitting, one at the head and the other at the feet, where the body of Jesus had lain. 13 Then they said to her, "Woman, why are you weeping?" She said to them, "Because they have taken away my Lord, and I do not know where they have laid Him." 14 Now when she had said this, she turned around and saw Jesus standing [there], and did not know that it was Jesus. 15 Jesus said to her, "Woman, why are you weeping? Whom are you seeking?" She, supposing Him to be the gardener, said to Him, "Sir, if You have carried Him away, tell me where You have laid Him, and I will take Him away." 16 Jesus said to her, "Mary!" She turned and said to Him, "Rabboni!" (which is to say, Teacher). 17 Jesus said to her, "Do not cling to Me, for I have not yet ascended to My Father; but go to My brethren and say to them, 'I am ascending to My Father and your Father, and [to] My God and your God.' "

He appeared to her first, even before going to see the Father. When She needs Him, Jesus is always there to support and strengthen His Bride, wherever she may be, to the ends of the earth.

The Bride often remains hidden. She's content with that because she dwells in "the Secret Place" (Psalm 91:1). But when called upon she can be revealed.

[Song of Songs 2:14 N.A.S.B.] 14 [BRIDEGROOM:] "O my dove, in the clefts of the rock, in the secret place of the steep pathway, let me see your form, let me hear your voice; for your voice is sweet, and your form is lovely."

Richard Wurmbrand was in prison in Romania when it was part of the communist, U.S.S.R. He recounts an experience:

...we were put in big common cells...dirty and [with] hunger and beatings...impossible to sleep with 200 in the same room...there were men of all kind of categories. There were formal generals of the Royal Army and capitalists and professors and there were rank-and-file: some peasants, some workers. And we had in our cell a peasant who knew his Bible well, but except the Bible he probably had never read a book. And his ambition was to win for Christ a professor of the Royal Academy of Science who was in the same cell. Now he did not know how to explain many things. The professor put questions he did not know the answers to, and he said, "Sir, I don't know all these things, but I know: I walk with Jesus; I talk with Jesus." "Go away!"

The circle of prisoners were around. "Go away! What lies do you tell us that you *walk* with Jesus? Jesus has lived 2000 years ago in Palestine. If I would show you a globe you could not point to where Palestine is. How can you walk with Jesus? He's dead since 2000 years, and even if it would be as you Christians say that he's somewhere in heaven, the heaven is also far away, millions of light years away. You can't walk with Jesus. You can't talk with Jesus." And he replied, "You might be right in your thinking, but I walk with Jesus. I talk with Jesus. I see Jesus." Now the professor was really indignant: "You dare to say that you see Jesus!" "Yes sir. I see him." "Listen, you say that you see Jesus. How does Jesus look to you?" Wrathful? Indignant? Annoyed? Bored? Indifferent? Happy to see you? Or does he sometimes smile to you?!"

"Sir, how did you guess? He sometimes smiles to me." "*Jesus smiles to you!?!* What a stupid thing!" he said to all the prisoners around. "This man says that Jesus smiles to him. Jesus smiles to you?" "Yes he does." "Show me how Jesus smiles."

I'm 80. That was the most beautiful episode in my life of 80 years. This farmer was very, very ugly, as we all were very ugly. We were hungry. We were beaten. We were like scarecrows. We were only skin and bones, dark circles around our eyes, and we were unwashed and in this uniform of a prisoner—we were very ugly, unimaginably ugly. And his face began to shine. …we have seen transfigurations as on Mt Tabor. The man was transfigured. He began to shine. And a gorgeous smile appeared on his face. I'm used to seeing smiles. My wife smiles much. I'm used to seeing smiles, but I've never seen such a beautiful smile. There was so much yearning in this smile and so much compassion for the lost soul whom he had near him and so much desire to see him saved and so much love and so much goodness. The whole splendor of heaven was in this smile. And the professor bowed his head and said, "Sir, you have seen Jesus."[8]

I have been saying from the beginning that the Bride grows up

---

8 "Transfiguration Testimony - Richard Wurmbrand" currently on YouTube

into the image of the glory of the Lord, as She sees it in the Mirror of the Word. She surpasses all limitations, gazing on that glorious image. I mentioned the wilderness, and the invaluable knowledge She personally receives there. It is there that She really learns to see Herself the way He does, fully. The old way of seeing Herself is unbolted and removed. She takes firm hold of the love-image of the Word She holds in Her heart. She can say,

[Song of Songs 6:3 N.A.S.B.] 3 "I am my beloved's and my beloved is mine, He who pastures his flock among the lilies."

[Song of Songs 7:10 N.A.S.B.] 10 "I am my beloved's, and his desire is for me.

And, like Jacob after his encounter with the angel of the Lord, She leaves totally different, no longer self-reliant. She walks carefully now, and She knows who She is.

And He calls Her out:

[Song of Songs 4:7-10 E.S.V.] 7 You are altogether beautiful, my love; there is no [blemish] in you. 8 Come with me from Lebanon, my bride; come with me from Lebanon. Depart from the peak of Amana, from the peak of Senir and Hermon, from the dens of lions, from the mountains of leopards. 9 You have captivated my heart, my sister, my bride; you have captivated my heart with one glance of your eyes, with one jewel of your necklace. 10 How beautiful is your love, my sister, my bride! How much better is your love than wine, and the fragrance of your oils than any spice!

Like her Bridegroom, she has now overcome in the wilderness and walks through all opposition. She is content now, steady, close to her Beloved, holding his arm, and she's rich. She comes out as the Lion.

Those who encounter her are taken aback. They had already begun calling her "most beautiful among women" (see Song of Songs 5:9 and 6:1). But eventually, they will be compelled to cry out:

[Song of Songs 8:5 NKJV] 5 Who is this coming up from the wilderness, leaning upon her Beloved? …

Others of the highest class ask about her in shock and awe:

[Song of Songs 6:10 E.S.V.] 10 "Who is this who looks down like the dawn, beautiful as the moon, bright as the sun, awesome as an army with banners?"

Just as the Father brought Eve through the Garden to Adam, he will escort the revealed Bride to His Son. That will be the brightest encounter the universe has ever seen, when the Bride stands before and takes the hands of the Bridegroom.

He will say to her, as Adam did

[Genesis 2:23 NKJV] 23 …"This is now bone of my bones and flesh of my flesh; She shall be called…"

He ALONE can define her, because she came out of him. And the pure, wedding veil will be drawn back, and we will see him:

[1 John 3:2 NKJV] 2 …it has not yet been revealed what we shall be, but we know that when He is revealed, we shall be like Him, for we shall see Him as He is.

When the Bride sees him in this face-to-face encounter, she will be seeing herself in his glory image again. Her final transformation will take place, like a flash of lightning.

When He sees her that way, he will be taken aback. He will exclaim,

[Song of Songs 6:5 NKJV] 5 Turn your eyes away from me, for they have overcome me….

What about her eyes caused him to jolt back like that? It is the Love in her eyes.

Remember what John saw of Jesus on the Island of Patmos. He said:

[Revelation 1:14 NKJV] 14 His head and hair [were] white like wool, as white as snow, and His eyes like a flame of fire

[Revelation 2:18 NKJV] 18 …These things says the Son of God, who has eyes like a flame of fire, and His feet like fine brass

[Revelation 19:12 NKJV] 12 His eyes were like a flame of fire, and on His head were many crowns…

What is that?

[Song of Songs 8:6 E.S.V.] 6 … love is strong as death, jealousy is fierce as the grave. Its flashes are flashes of fire, the very flame of the LORD.

The hottest possible flame is blue in color. It is this blue FIRE in the Bride's eyes that will cause the Lamb Himself to look down and away momentarily, stunned. That Love is unquenchable and incalculably valuable. It is her purity. The refinement process permanently melded that Love into her eyes. It devours anything. And she will be looking at him with it, eyes open wide.

[Song of Songs 8:7 E.S.V.] 7 Many waters cannot quench [this fire of] love, neither can floods drown it. If a man offered for love all the wealth of his house, [his offer] would be utterly despised [and rejected].

Her Bridegroom speaks into Her before she falls into his arms:

[Song of Songs 6:4-5 E.S.V.] 4 You are beautiful as Tirzah, my love, lovely as Jerusalem, awesome as an army with banners. 5 Turn away your eyes from me, for they overwhelm me—Your hair [your glory] is like a flock of goats leaping down the slopes of Gilead….

"My Dove who is complete is One; She is the One daughter of her mother, the pure Child of the One who gave birth to her."

–*King Jesus to His Bride*; Song of Songs 6:9, The Set Apart Book

More Life Changing Resources

Other Resources from David and Sonia O'Brien

- Free and Pure to Shine Mentorship - www.FreeAndPureToShine.com
- Other books by David or Sonia O'Brien
    - For Freedom
    - Shine ("Daughter of God, it is Your Time")
    - Heal the Sick
    - 25 Words, by Sonia O'Brien
    - Kingdom Rich, by Sonia O'Brien
- TheKingdomCourses.com
    - Reigning on The Kingdom Foundation
    - The For Freedom Summit Training
    - Religion-Proof Yourself
- The Path of Purity, by David O'Brien – www.PurityEducation.com
- ThePurityForum.com
    - A treasure chest of resources on freedom, relationships, marriage, intimacy, and family
    - The Purity Alliance
- Broadcasts
    - The Purity Forum Broadcast, by David O'Brien
    - Others at EmpowerMediaNetwork.com
- Podcasts - on Spotify
    - For Freedom Radio, by David O'Brien
    - Be The Light Podcast, by David O'Brien
    - Lovely Talk for Lovely Women, by Sonia O'Brien

Other Related Recommendations

- The Power School of Miracles: "His Beloved," by Ap. Charles Ndifon
- The Grace of Yielding, by Derek Prince
- The Marriage Covenant, by Derek Prince
- Does Your Tongue Need Healing, by Derek Prince
- Esther: Portrait of a Queen, audios by Derek Prince
- The Fire of Love – Praying the Song of Songs, with Mike Bikle
- The Sweetest Song, by Richard Wurmbrand

Empower Media Network – *EmpowerLiveTV.com*

www.BlueDiamondBookhouse.com

Free & Pure
to Shine
A 90 DAY, HIGH LEVEL,
MENTORSHIP EXPERIENCE
Find
Freedom!
Experience
Purity!
Shine in
Destiny!!!
Receive a free gift just
for considering!!
www.FreeAndPureToShine.com

The
KINGDOM
Courses
www.thekingdomcourses.com

FOR FREEDOM
How God Freed You from Slavery
DAVID O'BRIEN

BE
THE
LIGHT
PODCAST
BE FREE - BE PURE - BE THE LIGHT
On Spotify – with David O'Brien

Lovely Talk for Lovely
Women
A Podcast by Sonia O'Brien
On Spotify & Anchor

THE PURITY
FORUM
WWW.EMPOWERLIVETV.COM
DAVID O'BRIEN
DAILY - 9:30PM EST
(WED 6:30)

We welcome your positive feedback!!

If you have been immensely blessed by this work, and if you can, please send your video or written **TESTIMONIAL** to us via

www.BlueDiamondBookhouse.com
or
info@TheBondageBreaker.com

Thank you!

www.ingramcontent.com/pod-product-compliance
Lightning Source LLC
LaVergne TN
LVHW010918110826
845149LV00013B/2405

* 9 7 8 1 9 6 0 2 4 5 0 6 9 *